PRAISE FOR LAURA BULL

&

FROM INDIVIDUAL TO EMPIRE: A GUIDE TO BUILDING AN AUTHENTIC AND POWERFUL BRAND

"With small steps, big changes can occur. In this book, Laura shows you how to step by step cultivate and articulate not only a successful personal brand but an authentic and powerful one."

—**Shawn Achor**, *New York Times* best-selling author of
Big Potential and *The Happiness Advantage*

"Engaging and informative, this book is a treasure trove of golden nuggets."

—**Jim Loehr**, world-renowned performance
psychologist and best-selling author

"Laura Bull has achieved something remarkable. As the youngest executive to ever to work for Sony Music Nashville, she discovered early on what it really takes to establish an artist as a brand. Now she takes her knowledge to teach others how to build their own *powerful* and *authentic* brand."

—**Thomas R. Baldrica**, former Vice President of
Marketing, Sony Music Nashville

"In today's DIY music environment, artists must not only create great music, they must also develop an authentic brand identity that resonates with fans. *Individual to Empire* provides insights and strategies for building a successful career in music, literature, or any field where communicating and influencing are key. A must-read!"

—**Denise Shackelford**, Attorney, The Primary Firm,
Assistant Professor, Recording Industry,
Middle Tennessee State University

from INDIVIDUAL *to* EMPIRE

A GUIDE TO BUILDING AN AUTHENTIC AND POWERFUL BRAND

LAURA BULL

RIVER GROVE
BOOKS

Published by River Grove Books
Austin, TX
www.rivergrovebooks.com

Distributed by River Grove Books

Design and composition by Omar Mediano
Cover design by Jennifer K. Beal Davis
Creative direction by Colson Horton of ADR Creative
Photography by Cameron Powell
Excerpt from Oprah Winfrey reproduced by permission and courtesy of Harpo, Inc. All rights reserved.
Excerpts from TED Talk, "The Happy Secret to Better Work" by Shawn Achor. TEDxBloomington, May 2011. Copyright (c) 2011. Reproduced by permission of TED. To watch the full talk, visit TED.com

Publisher's Cataloging-in-Publication data is available.

Print ISBN: 978-1-63299-261-1

eBook ISBN: 978-1-63299-262-8

First Edition

Dedicated to those broken down on the side of the road on the way to the next gig; it gets better.

CONTENTS

—ACKNOWLEDGEMENTS—

This book was merely an idea for many years before serendipity took over and placed the right people in my world at the right time. When I'm asked how long my book is, I often truthfully joke that I've written well over 100,000 words, but only about 50,000 good ones. Between moving, getting married, having a baby, teaching, consulting, and finishing a master's degree, this book could have been derailed into nonexistence without the undying support of my tribe. I want to thank the village, old and new, for helping me jump hurdles and for shaping my understanding of the cross section between the human experience and marketing.

First, a sincere thanks to Dr. Janet Harris. She helped me, quite literally, find my voice. She believed in my idea and, even though I had zero writing experience, helped me develop this passion project into reality. Her consistent reassurance from the first page to the last is the only reason this book exists. A simple thank-you is not adequate. Also, I must thank Dr. Anthony Picchioni for busting open my egocentric predicament, Dr. Kimberley Monden for introducing positive psychology, Dr. Charlotte Barner for transforming my narrative, and the late Dr. Gerald Perkus for reminding me of the true meaning of the American dream.

Thank-you to the Sony Music greats who are pioneers and my personal heroes: Tom Baldrica, Tanya Welch, John Grady, Margie Hunt, Deb Haus, Mike Kraski, Butch Waugh, Heather McBee, and

Joe Galante. I enjoyed every late night and early morning, every ounce of stress, and every celebration, because I was able to learn firsthand from these extraordinary leaders. Together, we made a few dreams come true. I can never repay them for the immeasurable experiences both professional and personal.

A heartfelt thanks to everyone on my team: Barbara Norris, Cindy Birne, Jennifer K. Beal Davis, Colson Horton, Cameron Powell, Brenna Mader, Omar Mediano, Scott Safford, Michael A. Ransom, Gigi Stone Woods, Brian Apunda, Justin Branch, Jen Glynn, Sally Garland, Karen Cakebread, Emily Maulding, Tiffany Barrientos, O'Licia Parker-Smith, and everyone at Greenleaf Book Group. This phenomenal group shared their passions and their immense talents, and this project wouldn't be the same without any of them.

A big thank-you to my Dark and Stormies: Mary Harris, Mary Guthrie, Bonnie Bazley, Liz Grote, Pam Zeko, Sean Gilder, Sarette Albin, and Johnnie Mays. This group of talented writers, from poets to novelists, keeps me on my toes, triggers my creativity, and holds me accountable for what and how I write. The endless laughter and encouragement have pushed me past some serious writer's block many times and if you look closely, you will see each of them sprinkled throughout the book.

A shout-out to my girl tribe spread about the country: Tara, Mimi, Jessica, Capucine, and all my Nashville and Dallas girlfriends. They've each seen me at my best and my worst, and they still root for me anyways. That's true friendship.

An eternal thank-you to my family. My parents, Ellis and Leta and Jerry and Donna, have instilled grit into my being from the onset. They taught me the importance of education and made sure I never questioned my ability to do anything I wanted in this world.

It is because of them I am passionate about what I do, and mostly fearless about how I do it.

A special thanks to my grandparents, Appaw and Roma, for the endless love. Thanks to my supportive and loving in-laws, Bill and Mary, for flying down to watch Baby Girl so I could write. And, a begrudging thanks to my big brother, Mike, who pushed me down the stairs on a pool raft headed straight for tile flooring when we were kids. Despite that little hiccup, he has since become my closest ally in this world. Oh, and he deserves an extra special thanks for marrying Adriene, who quickly became my best friend, and for my Nugget, Bug, and the little Prince.

And most of all, my world would be miserable without my husband, Michael, and our perfect little girl, Ainsley. Without even realizing it, they've made all my dreams come true.

PART I:
The Influencer

–1–

BEYONCÉ'S DUAL ROLE

• • • •

EXTERIOR: HOME DEPOT PARKING LOT—DAY

The parking lot is bustling with cars moving in and out of spaces and consumers heading for the entrance or pushing shopping carts filled with merchandise.

MOVING SHOT

The camera zooms in on a Bentley, sparkling in the sun, entering the parking lot and pulling into a stall near the back.

CLOSE-UP

On superstar BEYONCÉ KNOWLES-CARTER. She steps out of the Bentley in a form-fitting designer dress, shiny sunglasses, and Louboutin heels.

MOVING SHOT

The MUSIC BED begins to play "Run the World (Girls)" as Beyoncé struts past the rows of parked cars and enters the store.

INTERIOR: HOME DEPOT STORE—CONTINUOUS

A Home Depot employee in a burnt-orange vest greets Beyoncé with a shocked expression. The MUSIC BED continues.

EMPLOYEE #1

Hello! Can I . . . help you find something?

BEYONCÉ

No thanks.

(continues past the employee with a smile)

MOVING SHOT

Beyoncé continues on her quest through the store, stopping employees and shoppers in their tracks. She doesn't notice the commotion as she discovers the item she is looking for and heads to check out.

INTERIOR: HOME DEPOT CHECKOUT
COUNTER—CONTINUOUS

Again, the employee looks shocked and manages to sputter out her sentence.

EMPLOYEE #2:
Did someone help you today?

BEYONCÉ:
I found what I needed just fine. Thank you.

The checkout process ends, and they exchange pleasantries as Beyoncé walks out of the store. The sun becomes blinding and the screen dissolves to white.

DISSOLVE TO:

INTERIOR: BEYONCÉ'S LIVING ROOM—DAY

We find Beyoncé in an upscale living room. She is screwing in the faceplate of a new light switch dimmer.

CAMERA ANGLE OUT

The room light dims up and down as she plays with the switch on the wall. She smiles and walks over to join her husband and young children on the couch. They snuggle up, lean back, and start watching a movie together.

NARRATOR
Helping independent women everywhere build a more glamorous life.

The Home Depot: More saving. More doing.

FADE OUT

This imaginary commercial, which only exists in my head until someone shares my brilliance with Home Depot's advertising agency, illustrates two major brands uniting in a partnership that is mutually beneficial. Some may consider this a celebrity endorsement of a corporate brand, but that's the Don Draper 1960s view of marketing.

Beyoncé is a celebrity and the CEO of a multimillion-dollar company. She is also the product that company sells. Beyoncé is a person and a commodity. She's a brand, and in the twenty-first century, we call her a macro-influencer.

To begin, let's redefine the existing notion of the term influencer. Online bloggers are not the only influencers. Politicians, musicians, authors, actors, community leaders, clergy, and so many others are major influencers in their arenas and thus earn the title. Celebrities and noncelebrities alike are busy wielding influence over vast populations both on and offline. Consumers in the digital age are becoming more distant from their fellow neighbors, but they still crave and seek out personal connections. Even if relationships with influencers are only one-sided, over a television set, through the radio, or online, the consumer perceives a genuine connection. We will discuss the principles of influence, rhetoric, and how influencers are becoming more powerful than ever before, so that you may develop the skills needed to take advantage of the influencer phenomenon.

Beyoncé, Ellen DeGeneres, Martha Stewart, and Reese Witherspoon are all members of the same club. They are successful entrepreneurs and they are powerful influencers. Over time these women have become macro-influencers across all platforms, with the ability to speak with authority on a wide range of topics. Their stories, and many others I share in this book, will help you understand how they became successful influencers by taking a crucial first step. Every one of these wildly successful women turned inward before they burst out of the starting gate. They did the hard work of figuring out who they are in order to create their unique and powerful brands.

IN THE BEGINNING, THERE IS THE BRAND

Influencers don't achieve their success by accident—ever. For a rare few, the knowledge might be intuitive, but each one understands the concept of branding, even as it applies to themselves. What makes influencer branding unique from traditional branding is that the core product is a real person, not an inanimate object. Sure, a CEO could be emotionally attached to a company or a product, but they are still one step removed. When their product receives harsh criticism or they experience the sting of a failed partnership, it is not a direct hit. In Chapters 3 and 4, I share the secrets of positive psychology that not only help you protect yourself from the ups and downs of the business, but also factor heavily into the creation of your brand.

In my twenty-five-year career branding and marketing celebrity musicians, I have heard this protest countless times: "I don't need branding; I know who I am."

Do not be fooled. You may know exactly who you are, but you still need branding if you're going to market yourself—your product—successfully. Branding is about presenting your unique characteristics as a commodity. What are you selling? To whom? How will your consumer respond? Self-awareness is the first step to discovering a strong brand identity.

The late Apple founder Steve Jobs once said, "Your brand is the single most important investment you can make for your business." I believe this so deeply that I have made it my life's work to understand the complexities of branding people. I left Sony Music Entertainment after a decade in the marketing and artist development department—working with artists like Carrie Underwood, Brad Paisley, and Johnny Cash—to focus on helping a new onslaught of independent artists cultivate marketing strategies that could compete with the major record labels with a fraction of the budget.

To my surprise, I found that a solid marketing strategy was not what these artists needed. First they needed branding. They had no idea what key, sellable elements set them apart from the hundreds of others making music. They had no narrative foundation to support a marketing plan, and no amount of money or smarts can create success without one. How can you promote or advertise a product without truly knowing what is being sold?

Imagine a house built on unstable dirt instead of concrete. A weak brand will cause any business to crumble and crash over time and even faster in the face of a storm. So, I set out on a mission to help influencers develop their brand before they made the grave mistake of going public too early or losing valuable investments. Once a faulty product is launched, it can be nearly impossible to correct. I'd give examples, but you have never heard of them. Their names are relegated to music industry oblivion.

Unless you are completely oblivious to contemporary music, you've heard of Beyoncé, and this is the reason I've made her the star player in our imaginary commercial. If Home Depot approached Beyoncé with a $20 million offer to star in a series of TV spots, her initial reaction could be, "Absolutely not." How could you blame her? Home Depot is masculine and gritty. It is blue collar with a do-it-yourself mentality. This is not Beyoncé. She wouldn't be caught dead in a burnt-orange work vest.

Beyoncé is all that Home Depot is not: She is glamorous and high class and the queen of independent women everywhere. These descriptions are true to her personality and her music. She is a brilliant businesswoman, too. Partnering with a brand that is quite obviously the complete opposite could destroy her authenticity and possibly her entire career. Yes, even if that career is already as solid as Beyoncé's. Turning down $20 million, while painful, would still be the right decision.

However, if Home Depot refocuses the ad campaign to empower women, things get a lot more interesting. This now becomes a conversation about narrative. What's the new message they want to relay to consumers? The message in the fictional commercial is that Home Depot can empower women to become more independent. A woman, even a superstar, may be able to hire someone to change a light dimmer, but she doesn't have to. She may have a man in her life, but she doesn't need him to fix her problems. She may be wearing designer clothes, but she doesn't have to get dirty, if, of course, she doesn't want to. "Who runs the world? Girls!"

Now this partnership becomes a natural fit because Beyoncé doesn't have to change who she is. The narratives intersect at an authentic place for both parties. Like Home Depot's, the Beyoncé brand did not materialize out of thin air. It's based on a careful analysis of who she is and what she has to offer. For Home Depot, one of the key characteristics of the brand is supporting self-reliance. For Beyoncé, it's empowering independent women, something she's been doing since Destiny's Child. This new partnership reinforces the overall consistency of both brands. So, Beyoncé, go on and get Home Depot on the phone!

BRAND IDENTITY FOR THE INFLUENCER'S BUSINESS

A real, live, breathing person presents many challenges to creating a successful brand, challenges a product-based company simply would not face. There are psychological components that must be addressed and incorporated into an influencer's brand identity that are nonexistent for a typical product. These forces must help shape the brand as well as grow it over time. Failure to tap into the psychological components at the onset will spell disaster for anyone building a brand.

Influencers must learn to view themselves as a product. They need to be able to step back, remove their personal bias from the equation, and make sound business decisions. McDonald's golden arches can't think, and their french fries don't feel. They have a board of directors who study analytics, make projections, and develop strategies to increase their market share. Influencers, on the other hand, may have a very difficult time separating the creation of their product from the business of getting that product to the consumer. They tend to make shortsighted business decisions based on emotional or personal needs, and that typically leads to disaster. That's why the first thing a young influencer has to learn is how to distinguish between the self as a person and the self that is a commodity.

Influencers must also be okay with commercializing personal attributes. Public figures must be willing to be vulnerable, sharing their true selves in order to create a connection with their audience. But sometimes an artist's craft is so personal they don't want to taint the experience by turning their work into a commodity. In this case, my advice would be to go home and enjoy your work privately, and decide on another career path to pay the rent. For everyone else who doesn't believe that commercialism equates to selling out, read on, and you will learn how to identify your core brand and how to promote it publicly.

BRAND LONGEVITY

In my experience, outliers (top achievers who don't operate within society's so-called norms) struggle with finding purpose, confidence, and even happiness, like the rest of the population. They just tend to be affected on a larger scale due to the added public pressures. Competition is fierce, and pressures mount daily. Knowing and feeling comfortable with an authentic brand tends to help combat these serious distractions. I have found a direct correlation between confidence levels and time and effort spent on branding. This book will help define your unique definition of success and provide focus to achieve your long-term goals.

An influencer's brand is only as strong and as lasting as their grit, perseverance, and overall well-being. If the CEO of McDonald's becomes exhausted and burns out, the board will simply replace him or her, and the company will continue churning out Quarter Pounders. If, however, the CEO and the product are intertwined, the product tanks while the CEO is in recovery. The influencer succumbs to the stresses, a bad public narrative ensues, and the influencer fades away, along with the business they built.

Finally, most products don't have to change over time, but a human has no choice but to evolve. I often see fear in a client's eyes when I stress the importance of consistency in order to achieve brand loyalty. They feel stifled and pressured by the sudden need for long-term sustainability and wonder how they could possibly be the exact same person every single day for the rest of their lives. They assume consistency means the brand must be perfect at the onset and unchanging, which just happens to be impossible to achieve. Here's the key that will make all that undue stress evaporate: Evolution does not equal change.

When a brand evolves over time, the core brand remains constant. Since Nike launched the iconic Just Do It campaign in the 1980s, the core brand has not changed. They have maintained consistency. Yes, they have evolved alongside the consumer, modernized their product lines, and updated minor narratives, but their core brand has not changed.

Beyoncé has evolved just like all the other macro-influencers discussed throughout this book. Her musical styling and image have matured, and the themes in her music have become more family oriented as she has become a mother and wife. But her core brand pillars have remained consistent since her first Destiny's Child album. An influencer must find the delicate balance between consistency for the sake of brand loyalty and evolution for authenticity and sustainability. In Chapter 10 you will learn how to recognize which core elements can be viable for years to come and how to methodically evolve.

If an influencer is armed with an evolution strategy, they may avoid a complete rebrand, although sometimes evolving a brand is not enough. At some point in an influencer's career, it may be necessary for a rebrand. This process is tedious and expensive and often unsuccessful. External factors, such as competition and the marketplace, and internal factors, such as life experiences and psychological transformations, could make a rebrand unavoidable. Since crystal balls do not reveal this information in advance, influencers must be vigilant to avoid surprises that could result in serious career damage. The tools I give you in this book will go a long way toward helping you avoid a total rebrand down the road.

CREATING YOUR BRAND STATEMENT

The developmental stages of an influencer's brand require a lot of introspection, analysis, and practice. This can take some time. The process cannot be rushed or forced. But fear not. One day everything will make sense and the aha moment will arrive.

There is also no right or wrong answer; what is right for you may work only for you. We could not build your brand by copying Beyoncé's because a) it already exists only for her and b) you are a beautiful, exceptional soul that deserves your own moment to shine. In order to pull together all the elements that show off your unique qualities, I will give you tasks to complete as we move along together. Answer truthfully and take your time; no one will see your answers. Only you know if you are being honest with yourself. The objective is to know your brand (yourself) so thoroughly, so deeply, that these exercises will become second nature. This ingrained knowledge will help you face difficult day-to-day decisions while enjoying peace of mind and clear direction for your goals.

After you have completed all the exercises in this book, you will embark on a quest to develop your own brand statement. Regular businesses have mission statements, which are really brand statements that communicate who they are, what they stand for, and what they do. A brand statement is a mission statement for influencers. Here are some examples of corporate mission statements:

● ● ● ●

DARDEN RESTAURANTS

TO NOURISH AND DELIGHT EVERYONE WE SERVE.

FORD MOTOR COMPANY

WE ARE A GLOBAL FAMILY WITH A PROUD HERITAGE PASSIONATELY COMMITTED TO PROVIDING PERSONAL MOBILITY FOR PEOPLE AROUND THE WORLD.

NIKE

TO BRING INSPIRATION AND INNOVATION TO EVERY ATHLETE IN THE WORLD.

● ● ● ●

A brand statement is a personalized mission statement that provides purpose and focus. Some clients work it into their website or bio, while others write it on a sheet of paper and hang it above their desks as a daily reminder. I have found that a brand statement provides the needed focus for an influencer and the team that supports them in order to maintain high levels of energy, confidence, and perseverance over the long haul.

Your brand statement must be generic enough to allow for growth, but specific enough to tell the audience who you are and why you matter. It must be unique enough to separate you from the competition, and it must factor in your personality and accentuate marketable elements that will remain authentic over time.

Corporations spend millions of dollars every year to create and protect their brands, which are an invaluable asset. You won't spend the millions, but you will put in the time and energy, and you should be every bit as protective of the brand that will carry you to long-term success.

If all this sounds a bit overwhelming, don't worry. You don't have to hit the ground running. The following chapters will guide you through the process with advice on branding strategies and, most important, a user-friendly tutorial on my brand matrix, a tool I developed that will help you transform your personality and product into a successful business. Together we will discover your target audience and find your unique position in the marketplace. We will discuss how the image you present through your brand must represent you authentically, and how to develop a positive narrative while avoiding the bad ones. We will look at the differences between private and public narratives and how they work together to create a cohesive story. Step by step, you will learn the subtle art of evolving a brand.

By the end of this book, you will understand the branding process like a pro. Then, armed with your unique brand built to weather any challenges you encounter as a world-class influencer, you will be ready to take the next step and focus on marketing, advertising, and promotion. Marketing strategies are the topic for another book, but, lucky you, I have included my favorite go-to marketing resources on my website at laurabull.com to further your knowledge and propel your newly minted brand to the masses. My hope is that by the time you are ready for that information, you should be well on your way to creating your own business empire just like Beyoncé.

—2—

ALL STORIES ARE CONNECTED

● ● ● ●

"All stories are connected. And there's nothing that anyone who's living on earth has ever felt, or known, or experienced on a soul level that hasn't been felt, or known, or experienced by someone else. . . . I define a master as someone who has fully stepped in and owned the full progress and trajectory of their life. But hearing stories told from the mouths of people who know how to live, how to course correct, how to keep going, how to never quit, how to rejoice in the good times and have faith in the bad . . . Those people are masters. Anyone who can do that is a master. And their ability to share their stories only helps the trajectory of others who listen."

—Oprah, the queen influencer herself

Masters become influencers only when they share their stories in a way that makes others relate on an intimate level. Who better to teach us how than one of the most influential masters of the twenty-first century, Oprah Winfrey. The building blocks she laid are the very same bricks that other influencers must use to build their own foundations. She has become part of our lexicon: a household name. Her antics linger decades after airing: "You get a car! And, you get a car!" But, she didn't just stumble and fall into the homes of American housewives, nor did she cast a spell for implicit trust.

In fact, Oprah's start was rocky. The 1970s proved a difficult time for African-Americans to break into television, and she lost her first large-market coanchor position because she was considered boring and uptight. This didn't seem like a promising start, and it doesn't sound like the woman who became the voice for suburban, stay-at-home mothers in fly-over states.

But Oprah spun that defunct Baltimore anchor position into a megabrand by finding a better-suited niche when she was reassigned to a local talk show. That major-market talk show morphed into a Chicago morning show and then into a nationally syndicated one-hour program. Oprah did not take her new visibility for granted. She used this national platform to discuss the social issues she experienced firsthand, and with sincerity and kindness, offered her audience a place to feel included and heard. She publicly acknowledged her flaws and presented herself as the work-in-progress she has continued to be. Her audience members, conceding their own ever-evolving journeys, were all ears and all hearts, because they identified with her.

Once this personal connection became virtually unbreakable, Oprah's popularity soared to new heights. She solidified her brand as someone seeking enlightenment and betterment. No matter how she slipped, on weight fluctuations or controversial issues, the audience remained ever forgiving and trusting. She was always a work-in-progress, just like them. She tackled grim human realities like AIDS and sexual assault with respect, and created a platform for members of society and issues that had previously been labeled taboo. She embraced these themes with a spiritual, not religious, undertone, which avoided polarization.

Self-forgiveness, self-awareness, and self-efficacy are her brand cornerstones. Without them, Oprah would have been just another woman on television sharing sound bites with her audience. With them, she had a unique voice that manifested across magazines, books, and movie roles. With her world-famous book club, she pioneered the phenomenon of branded communities, which are groups of consumers who form around their loyalty for a specific brand. It is her strength in developing these communities of like-minded individuals, both through her television audience and online, that solidifies her as such a powerful, influential figure.

If Oprah loved it, her audience loved it. It sold, and sold a lot. Unfortunately, for the beef industry in the late 1990s, the reverse was also true. Her comments on the repulsive manufacturing practices of the industry created a backlash that brought with it the lowest beef prices in a decade. Just a few comments on just one episode brought an entire industry to its knees. America witnessed firsthand what advertisers had known for years: the tremendous influence of the O.

Today she runs a media empire, the Oprah Winfrey Network (OWN), and her extensive list of businesses spans multiple industries. Recently, after purchasing a large share of Weight Watchers, she stepped into the role of their spokesperson. Overnight, counting points while still succumbing to carb cravings became cool again, and the company's value more than tripled. This authority over everyday consumers is the essence of the term influencer. So, with the majority of Oprah's numerous successes offline, why do so many marketers overwhelmingly refer to only online personalities as influencers? An online platform is merely a conduit to disseminate an influencer's message, and therefore a term that seeks to encompass Oprah and other business moguls like her should be stretched to include all media platforms.

TYPES OF INFLUENCERS

The world of online influencer marketing is relatively new. Terminology is varied, inconsistent, and way too narrow in scope. For instance, there are many powerful influencers, like Angelina Jolie and George Clooney, who do not even operate on social media. This defies the widely accepted interpretation of the term influencer.

Let's take another stab at defining that term.

An influencer is anyone, conducting business online and/or offline, who can manipulate their consumer base to similar viewpoints based on a perceived personal connection.

Depending on the source, there are varied levels of influencer power. I concur with John Lincoln, a social media professor at the University of California San Diego, who sees three main categories: micro-influencer, subject-matter expert, and macro-influencer. These levels are based on how influencers operate their business at each stage. Most other categories like nano-influencer and mega-influencer are based on follower counts online, which would not apply to the offline operations nor is it a reliable way to measure the viability of a business.

The celebrity personalities that we discuss in this book fall into the macro category, but here's the catch. They all had to make their way through the other stages first. Oprah took two decades to rise from micro-influencer to macro-influencer. Just as a star is not born overnight, neither is an influencer.

The micro-influencer is at the first step. They have a small network, but more importantly, a close one. They hold influence over friends, family, and community, whether local, like the PTA president, or online, like a Facebook group administrator. A micro-influencer gains power by earning trust one person at a time, which can be a long and tedious process, but necessary all the same. When Taylor Swift was embarking on her career, she responded to each and every fan comment on her Myspace page, forging a personal human connection that laid the solid foundation of her future stardom. Micro-influencers exploit the perception of a real human relationship, and their early adopters begin to share the micro-influencer's message with those outside of the close-knit circle.

Next, the micro-influencer is propelled into the role of a subject-matter expert. The foundation has been laid; the core fan base has been cemented. The audience no longer consists of Mom and Dad and baby brother singing along from the front row. The club goes from twenty close friends to hundreds—maybe even thousands—of consumers (because let's face it . . . Mom and Dad got in free). This is the phase where the influencer must prove they are among the best in their field in order to gain attention and admiration from those beyond their inner sanctum. If the public is deprived and aching for your product, this phase will come rather quickly. From there, it's a natural progression to macro-influencer.

Lincoln describes the macro-influencer as someone who has "significant influence reaching a variety of subjects, industries, and demographics." The list of macro-influencers is as long as it is varied. They dwell in every industry, from politics to Silicon Valley, and from entertainment to lifestyle specialists. Macros are celebrity chefs, photographers, reporters, authors, and the list goes on. The Kardashians and Jenners are macros, for example, because they can influence a mass following to buy luxury vacations, lip gloss, designer clothing, and even a Carl's Jr. burger. And of course, Oprah is in the upper echelon of the macro category. Just about everyone on the planet knows her brand and it is overwhelmingly adored. Her influence is so substantial, people claim an appearance on her show was the catalyst to Barack Obama's election to the presidency.

There are successful influencers at every level—micro, expert, and macro—and they come from all areas of our cultural life. The secret to surviving your own rise up the ladder is to recognize the necessity of growing each level at your own pace and to grasp the ability to exert authentic, influential power at any stage. A micro-influencer can celebrate a fantastic small business, pulling in millions a year by taking the time to connect with its audience.

Achieving influencer status at any level means that you have achieved brand loyalty.

BRAND LOYALTY

When you're building a business, brand loyalty is everything. If an influencer is dedicated to making each person feel a personal connection, the consumer will become brand loyal and the influencer will gradually grow to the next level. The wider and more dedicated the audience becomes, the more successful the brand. This is the reason buying Likes on Facebook and followers on Twitter will get a business into trouble fast. If the foundation isn't real, the house will collapse, and the buyer will move on to the next influencer, of which there are plenty.

The bottom line is that the term influencer is no longer synonymous with celebrity in the twenty-first century. Someone can be a celebrity and lack the ability to influence or inspire brand loyalty, and someone who is not a household name can be an influencer.

> **All Celebrities ≠ Influencers**
> **and**
> **All Influencers ≠ Celebrities**

Many mini Oprahs roam among us. Forms of public communication, from television to the Internet, have made it easier for everyone around the world to connect. It is the job of the influencer to discover the best way to make those connections, share their point of view, and optimize the potential for a substantial revenue stream along the way. In Darwinian fashion, only the fittest survive and thrive in such a diverse and saturated market.

THE PSYCHOLOGY OF INFLUENCE

To influence an audience effectively, we must understand the art of persuasion, and to understand the art of persuasion, we have to look at the basic principles of rhetoric. From the great Greek philosophers and orators Aristotle and Cicero to twentieth-century world leaders like Churchill and Kennedy, the power of logos (appeal to logic), pathos (appeal to emotion), and ethos (appeal to ethics) has been central to their narratives. The more adept the influencer is in their appeal to logic, emotion, and ethics, the more successful they are.

See the box below to get a quick crash course in rhetorical appeals before moving on to influencing principles.

RHETORICAL APPEALS

The musician Sarah McLachlan and the British Columbia Society for the Prevention of Cruelty to Animals (BC SPCA) partnered for a commercial that has become notorious for causing emotional distress while successfully enticing viewers to open their wallets. Why is it so influential? Get some tissues, take a deep breath, and watch the commercial at:

https://www.youtube.com/watch?v=9gspElv1yvc

Logos = using facts and reason to persuade an audience

The words on the screen: "Every single hour in British Columbia, an animal is violently abused. 3,000 animals were rescued last year." If the commercial relied only on logos, would it be as effective? Would it be as effective if you removed the words? The viewers need the facts to determine the seriousness of the problem.

Ethos = proving credibility or character of the persuader

Sarah McLachlan is the persuader and she is an animal lover (as she pets the dog in her lap). She is a staunch supporter of the charity (as she mentions how inexpensive it is to help an animal in need). She knows how easy it is to make a difference and is asking the viewer to join her pursuit.

Pathos = persuading by eliciting an emotional response

This advertisement smacks the viewer with pathos: the horrendous slow-motion images of abused animals, confined to cages, with their bleeding and scarred faces and pleading eyes; the terms that Ms. McLachlan uses, like hope, innocent, and love, as she says, "Will you be an angel for a helpless animal?" Well, when you put it that way!

Then comes the not-so-subliminal music bed with a gentle stab to the heart and the promise of safer times ahead "in the arms of the angel." Oh, wait, I'm the angel! By giving money to this foundation I'm literally wrapping a defenseless puppy in my arms and comforting it. Well played, McLachlan, well played. Here's my money.

Ad campaigns and speeches are just a few examples that utilize a mix of all three appeals to achieve their persuasive agenda, but as you can see, this one leans heavily on pathos. Check out the list of great speeches and further reading on rhetoric at the end of this book if you'd like to dive deeper.

Understanding rhetorical appeals is the first step to understanding the psychology of influence. Next, a strong influencer must cultivate the persuasive techniques hidden within the message. Influence expert Robert Cialdini wrote about the six key principles of influence in his 1984 book *Influence: The Psychology of Persuasion*. These fundamental principles are just as relevant today as they were decades ago and must factor into the creation of an emerging brand.

RECIPROCITY

Reciprocity in any relationship means the exchange of positives, enabling both parties to benefit from each other. The actual definition claims it must be "equally beneficial" or "mutually beneficial," but in my experience it doesn't necessarily have to be equal so long as it is not less than. A response can be more beneficial to one party, but a response cannot be less beneficial if the relationship is to be maintained. If a friend gives me a birthday present, I may reciprocate by doing the same for her, or I may reciprocate by helping her land a job. The value of one is greater than the other, although one could say the sentiments behind each are equal.

Influencers like Oprah must reciprocate with both consumers and sponsors to incite a positive reaction. When Oprah shares a recipe with her viewers, they buy a copy of *O* magazine. When she recommends a book, they follow her online. And then, even though she has already curated content that she knows her fans will enjoy, she rewards them again by giving away cars or her favorite things each year.

Sponsors supply those favorite things free of charge in exchange for the promotional value, which, if Oprah is involved, is astronomical. Oprah doesn't have to pay for the goods, she makes her audience happy, and she makes the sponsors happy. Win, win, win.

To develop a positive relationship with their followers, influencers must ask themselves what content they can provide that is not only entertaining, but also useful and appreciated. A common mistake I see is influencers concentrating solely on promoting themselves and forgetting the importance of reciprocity. "I'm appearing on TV today, tune in!" "My new album is out now, buy it!" "Don't forget to buy tickets to my show tonight!" Me, me, me.

Plan out a ratio of give and take that enables you to offer your followers something in return. The rewards can be giveaways, or acknowledgment, or free content. I use a 3:1 ratio with my clients: For every single ask, they must give three times. And, don't think money is an issue. Swift didn't have to spend a dime responding to those Myspace messages. Be creative!

COMMITMENT AND CONSISTENCY

Consistency is such a major component to a burgeoning brand that I have devoted all of Chapter 10 to the topic. Commitment to building your brand, and consistency within your message about that brand, is paramount.

The one thing that all successful brands have in common is that they have remained consistent.

Advertisers used to say that it took an average of three impressions before a consumer acted. Nowadays, due to information overload, many say that number is closer to ten. An impression is the point at which a consumer encounters a brand, either by hearing or sight. One impression could include hearing a song on the radio, seeing an ad on Facebook, or watching a performance on the *Today* show. There are many different ways in which a brand can earn impressions. When I say a consumer acts, I don't necessarily mean with a purchase. The action could be as simple as becoming intrigued enough to Google for more information. The greater number of impressions earned, the greater the chance for success, but only if the consumer has not seen conflicting or confusing information.

Oprah shows commitment by constantly churning out content for her audience and she is consistent with what she offers. This develops a strong fan base because the audience knows what to expect. They turn to Oprah when they need motivation, and she never disappoints.

For a new influencer, it's important to set social media schedules, use a limited number of rotating publicity photos, and make sure the message is the same across all communication platforms. One way to do this is through adaptable design, using one main visual across all assets. For my clients, that means to use the album cover design elements, such as font, graphics, and/or photos, as their social media cover photos, on their merchandise, on their websites, and anywhere else a fan may come in contact with their brand. It means the same font should be used as their backdrop on the *Today* show. It means they use the same photos and imagery until the next album comes out. Even something as subtle as using the same font will help the consumer connect the dots between that image and that influencer.

Of course, long-term brand consistency goes beyond font choices and social media schedules. We'll get to that later.

SOCIAL PROOF

Social proof refers to the psychological need to copy the behavior of others in order to feel included. One of our most basic biological requirements is the need to belong—to feel acceptance and trust those who are closest to us. The human race has always gathered in tribes and clans to increase the chance of survival. People feel safe in numbers. So, it is no surprise that consumers look to their co-consumers in order to confirm an influencer's legitimacy and establish trust.

Oprah has been off daytime television for a while now, yet she still maintains her branded online communities. Other influencers, like Ellen, throw their names on merchandise offerings like Apple does with their logo. When we walk into a coffee shop anywhere in the country, nearly every person is working on a Mac, listening to Beats, and talking on an iPhone. The Apple logo is practically synonymous with Starbucks. Apple must be a great company if so many other consumers have bought in, right? The brain processes this connection subconsciously yet creates a conscious desire to purchase the product.

One of the first statistics that consumers notice about the online presence of an influencer is the number of followers or Likes they have earned from other consumers. That number assures them that the influencer is worth their time. Of course, social proof makes it harder for an influencer to gain footing early on when their circle of influence is small, but it allows for a growth pattern that should increase exponentially as their business continues to thrive. So even though the beginning stages may feel like trudging through a mud pit, a tipping point is on the horizon. Just concentrate on getting those Likes up, keeping the comments flowing, and interacting with other influencers with the same target market as yours.

LIKING

Do not confuse social proof and liking. One is about belonging to a tribe, the other is about being drawn to those who are like-minded. Consumers are drawn to influencers who they perceive are like them: those who share the same values, lifestyle, wants, and needs. This is why it is paramount for an influencer to understand their consumer's demographics and focus on the target market that will accept and appreciate what they have to offer. Oprah found her niche with the housewives of middle America. She shared her struggles and her triumphs, and the audience concluded that Oprah was a lot like them. This forged a solid connection and grew her audience quickly.

This subconscious bond, like the one Oprah forged, helps influencers on two fronts. First, sharing her real self early on encouraged the natural growth and development of her audience. Oprah's vulnerability, openness, and kindness on certain issues attracted viewers who agreed with her viewpoint. Second, because Oprah really is like her audience, she understands deeply what the audience will want and enjoys giving it to them. Oprah knew that her audience wanted to become more self-aware, so she cultivated programming around that idea, thereby reinforcing her own brand. It's cyclical goodness. This doesn't work just for Oprah. This is a template for all influencers. Share your real self to find your audience. Know what to give your audience to keep them coming back.

The tiniest detail can draw people together in mutual admiration. People outside of Texas don't always understand the roots of Texas pride, but let me tell you, it runs deep. I am a daughter of the Texas Revolution, as my ancestors were in this state during the siege on the Alamo. That's something that provides serious street cred around here. When I found out that Sandra Bullock chose to make Austin her home, I just knew we could be best friends.

That tribal inclination worked the same way in my real life. I found my childhood best friend, Jessica, because she wore a Paula Abdul tour shirt to class one day in elementary school. "Forever Your Girl" was my jam, and I knew that if she had gone to the concert, we would get along just fine. The ensuing conversation about our mutual respect of Ms. Abdul, at ten years old, led to an almost thirty-year, cross-country friendship. All because we liked the same artist.

The best advice with this one is, just be yourself! Really. So simple!

AUTHORITY

An influencer with authority will command attention. This is why a subject-matter expert will always come before a macro-influencer. Become an expert in the field and others will take note. From the time a baby is born they look to authority figures to learn how to act, think, and feel. When a stylist with an A-list clientele raves about the new Christian Siriano collection, consumers will trust the advice and make a purchase from that collection. They will accept that Nike is the best clothing line for athletes when they see Serena Williams win her twenty-third Grand Slam while sporting the swoosh.

When the queen of daytime accepted the Cecil B. deMille Award at the 2018 Golden Globes, she gave a powerful speech about race, gender, and the pursuit of justice. The aftermath spurned an #OprahforPresident crusade. As the first African-American female recipient, during the ignition of the #MeToo movement, Oprah used the opportunity to teach and inspire, and in the process, just happened to reestablish herself as an authoritative figure. She shared historical facts and personalized them, she spoke with her signature, booming voice, and she called on the people of America to fight for justice.

No one ever declared Oprah an expert; she made herself one. If you believe you have a solid foundation as an expert or have the best product in the market, then others will believe in you too. Put your resume front and center and learn the delicate art of self-promotion. Speak with confidence and purpose to incite a strong following. And, be wary of old adages like "fake it 'til you make it." This is great advice up to a point, and then it can get you into hot water. A teenage fashion blogger who has yet to be accepted into Parsons School of Design may not make much headway giving suggestions for cocktail party attire but may do better focusing on the best trends for prom or the most comfortable ensemble to wear at a pep rally.

SCARCITY

The principle of scarcity suggests that people are more valuable when they are less available. From a business standpoint, this principle hearkens to the basic economic correlation between supply and demand: If the supply is withheld, then the demand increases, and vice versa. The marketing gurus at the Walt Disney Company utilize scarcity each time they pull *The Little Mermaid* out of the vault "for a limited time only." By withholding titles on a rotating basis, Disney ensures that parents will snatch up available titles in fear of disappointing their children by missing out.

We see influencers use scarcity by keeping certain personal details private or by boycotting social media altogether. Oprah rarely shares details of life at home with Stedman, and she disappears behind the scenes for months at a time. All Oprah all the time would lead to a quick audience burnout factor that even the queen herself couldn't avoid.

Another prime example of scarcity is Adele boycotting Spotify during her album release in the fall of 2015. By withholding the availability of free streaming and going against the industry norm, she risked upsetting her massive loyal fan base, who were forced into purchasing the music. The gamble paid off. Adele sold over three million units in one week in the United States alone. Billboard reported that such a massive feat was "the largest single sales week for an album since Nielsen began tracking point-of-sale music purchases in 1991." In a declining sales market, in a struggling music industry, Adele manipulated the principle of scarcity to crush every other artist on the scene.

Building demand is the same as building hype. Oversharing every aspect of your life forty times a day suggests desperation and leads to follower fatigue. A little secrecy adds indisputable intrigue. Keep them guessing, and they will tune in for more. Lastly, don't be afraid to take time away from major platforms or social media. The audience will still be there when you return.

THE BONUS SEVENTH PRINCIPLE/ THE UNITY PRINCIPLE

Robert Cialdini updated his initial six principles to include a seventh, which he calls the "Unity Principle." This states that when we identify ourselves in others, we are more influenced by them. The seventh principle hinges on the moral fabric and values that are consistent with our own beliefs. The liking principle is surface-level: "I like you because we like the same thing." Unity is a deeper shared identity: "We are both Irish Catholic, and therefore, we are part of the same tribe."

In her 2018 Golden Globe Awards acceptance speech, Oprah effortlessly provided all viewers with a shared identity:

> "In my career, what I've always tried my best to do, whether through television or film, is to say something about how men and women really behave. To say how we experience shame, how we love, how we rage, how we fail, how we retreat, persevere, and how we overcome. I've interviewed and portrayed people who've withstood some of the ugliest things life can throw at you, but the one quality all of them seem to share is the ability to maintain hope for a brighter morning, even during our darkest nights."

Oprah has been successful sharing an identity with her audience because, ironically, she avoids specificity by digging to the lowest common denominator. For instance, she has done many shows on spirituality, while avoiding focus on a specific religion. This helps her maintain a generic moral code that could apply to any faith. The shared belief was specific enough to speak to the audience, but generic enough to stave off any discrimination, or even worse, backlash.

RECIPROCITY, COMMITMENT AND CONSISTENCY, SOCIAL PROOF, LIKING, AUTHORITY, SCARCITY, AND UNITY

The cohesive combination of these principles will become the foundational support for any influencer and should remain in the forefront of business strategy from beginning to end. Influencers should set their goals, use persuasive techniques to accomplish them, and make sure to hit the refresh button if one of the methods is not yielding the expected response or outcome. Implementing the persuasive techniques should be uncomplicated for a well-developed short-term strategy, as this case study will illustrate.

CASE STUDY

IMPLEMENTATION OF PERSUASIVE TECHNIQUES

I'm a subject-matter expert carving out a niche for myself in the world of fashion. I'm a stylist by trade, not a designer, and the cornerstones of my brand are laid-back, frugal, fun, and a little retro with a dash of class. These elements would also be a good representation of my personality. My target audience is confident women in their twenties who are starting out in the workplace (limited budget and idealistic), college-educated (in a profession that requires an elevated and polished look), and who value independence and a balanced lifestyle. They strive for uniqueness and ease.

SHORT-TERM GOALS

To increase my perceived expertise, increase my Instagram following, and acquire a large retail partnership.

MARKETING STRATEGY

- Partner with a regional publication for a weekly fashion spread (authority). The editorial will be a weekly collection of my daily Instagram photos (consistency) showcasing articles of clothing from national retailers (reciprocity) used in my daily life (liking/unity).
- Tag the retailers and publication in each Instagram post. In the fashion spread, share the best Likes/Comments from each post (social proof) and which items are from which retailers (reciprocity).
- Maintain focus of all posts to the selected articles of clothing that are currently on sale and those that scream my aesthetic/brand (liking/scarcity).

continued

OUTCOME

This one short-term strategy—and there will be many at any given time—will jump-start my persuasive campaign and help create legitimacy and maintain influencer identity. This identity formation is created by sharing authentic content my consumers will value.

ANALYTICAL STAGE

For this campaign, I will analyze growth and response rate on a weekly and monthly basis.

If I find that interaction is low, the remedy is to tweak the area after trial-and-error assessment. For instance, the publication may have a different demographic than the one that would respond best to the influencer brand, or maybe that publication hasn't done a great job of enticing consumer interaction. If one of these is the cause of low growth, then I would seek out a new partnership. Constantly building and rebuilding strategy is the only way to succeed.

THE INFLUENCER'S VOICE

Establishing a unique voice that will resonate with an audience is vital. Think of your voice as the medium that presents you to the public. That's no minor detail. The discovery process for this voice is imperative to the early stages of brand development, yet it may take time to accomplish. Don't rush through this part of the process. Every wrong turn will tell you which path is the correct one.

A songwriter must uncover their musical or thematic style, a novelist their tone. A politician must decide what they stand for and how to best communicate that vision, a photographer their viewpoint. Tone, purpose, and style are just a few potential elements that will help define a strong voice. Are you informal or formal, classic or modern, thoughtful or brash? How do you use phrasing and cadence? What is your attitude or character? How can you communicate that voice to your audience?

True creatives tend to enjoy the discovery process but often have difficulty with analysis, consistency, or objectivity after the fact. This is fine. This is expected. The trick is to learn how to remove bias from the equation and establish a lasting voice with focus and authenticity.

Compare the singsong preaching vocals of Dr. Martin Luther King Jr. with those of the forceful and foreboding Winston Churchill. Look at the difference between the spare prose of Ernest Hemingway and the lyrical F. Scott Fitzgerald or melodious John Mayer and rambling Bob Dylan. Search Twitter for @Wendys hilarious roasts and see how the style and tone differ from their competition. Now watch an Oprah Winfrey episode followed by Ellen.

When we look to Oprah, as we do for everything it seems, we see a well-defined voice using rhetorical appeals and persuasive techniques. She is classy, formal, introspective, and caring. She remains a source of positivity and hope. She treats her audience as equals in the quest for self-awareness. These intersecting components and her ability to use the principles of influence have made her one of the most recognizable influencers of all time. She is notable in her ability to remain true to herself, sharing her life journey, and connecting with her audience as no one has before her. She is undeniably a master.

WHAT'S NEXT?

To become a successful influencer, you must understand the three main categories of influencers, comprehend the time-proven rhetorical devices still used by the masters of influence today, and familiarize yourself with the psychology of influence as it applies to your business. Look through the steps below to discover your current status, your potential audience base, and your goals.

- Identify the type of influencer you are and why.
- Pinpoint the basic values of your brand.
- Write down who you think your audience is, based on who you are and what you are selling. What is the identity you share with your audience?
- Make a list of those who influence you. How did you discover them? What keeps you tuned in? Now identify the persuasive principles your favorite influencers use.

TIP: Remember the case study? Once you have finished this book and have a clear brand, you will begin working on your marketing strategy. Make a repeating appointment on your calendar called POI (Psychology of Influence) as a reminder to analyze each short- and long-term marketing strategy. On those days, look over each of the persuasive principles and create, elevate, or readdress the tactics you have been using to accomplish your goals. Think of it as monitoring the ROI (Return on Investment) of your POI.

3

THE LABEL OF SUCCESS

● ● ● ●

I pulled the heavy metal door open and climbed the large steps into the dark mahogany-paneled lounge area. The loud engine noise from the tour buses parked side by side reverberated off each other, and the thick stench of diesel followed me inside. As soon as the door slammed shut, there was serenity from the only noise that remained: the gentle vibration of the engine. All the curtains were drawn to black out the summer sun. I plopped down on the leather sofa and grabbed a water bottle from the drawer underneath, relieved to have a moment of silence and air-conditioning.

"Did you see today's chart?" He sat at the small side table and stared at his laptop screen, barely acknowledging my entrance.

This again?

"Not yet. I was trying to get through Chicago traffic to get here. What's it say?"

"I'm down five spins."

The smile plastered on my face was somewhere between annoyance and overselling. "Yes, but we are up spins for the week overall, so we'll be fine come Monday. You know Monday is the only radio chart that really matters."

"This is my last shot. You know that." His pleading eyes finally made their way from the computer screen to mine. "Two albums in, and five singles. If this doesn't work . . . We've just been hanging there on the other side of the Top 40 for weeks."

"Look, staring at that computer screen all day is distracting you from reality. Your stress is on another level." I waved my hand around our tiny, yet glamorous, enclosure. "Seriously, where are we right now?"

"A tour bus in Chicago." His quick response highlighted his growing agitation.

"Is that all?" I took a chug from the water bottle and leaned forward. "We are sitting on your tour bus, in one of the biggest cities in the country, where you will be opening for a multiplatinum superstar act in front of 20,000 people in about . . ." I looked at the time on my cell phone. " . . . four hours. They've spent good money to see you."

His silence suggested he hadn't wavered. I became more pointed. "Where were you a year ago?"

His tone became softer, almost sheepish. "On a van. Playing for fifty people in a small-town VFW hall."

"Exactly. Can you embrace that for a minute? Think about all those other musicians on the road tonight in their vans, pulling all-nighters to drive home after their gigs while you get to sleep cozy in your bunk.

We will always look further down the road, but we need to appreciate where we are along the way."

He rolled his eyes and went back to his computer, and although I felt like I was getting through, this conversation was déjà vu. Regardless, my priority now was to improve his mood as he prepared to entertain an amphitheater full of people. "Besides, did you see where the sales were this week?"

He shook his head no but refused to look up for fear of losing the argument. "You have a Top 10 most downloaded song this week. In all genres! That's the number we should focus on."

He stood up, defeated, and as he turned away, I caught the hint of a smile.

● ● ● ●

Positive spin is everything. Any publicist worth their salt massages a story to work to their client's best advantage. But this chapter is all about the internal positive spin. I can't be 100 percent sure, but I believe a version of this exchange has taken place with literally every artist I've ever worked with. The successful artist on his tour bus, whose name I'm not mentioning because I don't want you to think he is whiny, proves how easily the day-to-day grind of building a business can detract someone from their greater goals and lead to a quick burnout. My artist and friend is truly not a complainer. Such a reaction is normal human behavior. We tend to focus on others' successes and not see the effort that went into it. Therefore, we judge ourselves more harshly when we encounter insignificant setbacks. There are no overnight successes. Did Michael Phelps become the most awarded Olympian of all time simply by showing up? Would a Fortune 500 CEO earn that title straight out of college? Not a chance. The consumer may feel like the brand is an overnight success, but performers have been honing their craft for many years behind the scenes.

Malcolm Gladwell has become famous for the 10,000-Hour Rule, which he presents in his book *Outliers: The Story of Success*. The author, who explains marketing trends with an anamorphic view, claims that it requires 10,000 hours of practice to build any expertise. For perspective's sake, that's roughly three hours a day for ten years. Although there are other factors that Gladwell disregards, the fact that someone must develop their skill over time is exceedingly accurate.

A typical musician is going to spend countless hours producing songs only to play them live to a small room of people who may or may not be friends and family. They travel from state to state, in the middle of the night, to make their next show in a run-down bar. They visit each small-town radio station along the way, hoping to develop a friendship and an audience. On a good day, they make enough money to pay for gas and a hot meal. Night after night, this type of existence, literally living the job, can and will break a person's spirit, and it definitely stifles creativity. Only the fittest survive and thrive.

The band Fun released their record-breaking smash "We Are Young" in 2012, but most of their current audience is unaware that they formed in 2008, a solid five years prior, and released their first album without any acknowledgment. In addition, each member also played in other bands for years before finally coming together to form the Grammy Award–winning group.

Likewise, politicians dedicate many years of effort to gain power and stature before they earn a book deal and a national audience. Hillary Clinton left her hometown of Chicago to attend Yale Law

School. Beginning in the 1960s, she was a presidential campaign volunteer, worked for a US senator, and became an advisor during the Watergate scandal. After that she became a faculty member at the University of Arkansas law school. She went on to work at a law firm before embarking on a career in politics as the first lady of Arkansas. All of this happened before anyone had ever heard of Hillary or her husband, Bill, but the knowledge gleaned from the varied aspects of public service gave her the skill set to serve as a US senator. Following in the footsteps of Madeleine Albright and Condoleezza Rice, she became one of the highest-ranking women in the US government, serving as secretary of state under Barack Obama.

THE LABEL OF SUCCESS

Only those who have put in an Olympic athlete's level of effort could achieve such footing. It rarely has anything to do with talent. We can learn from the successes and struggles that the jittery artist on the tour bus and Hillary Clinton share along their quest for greatness. What made them get past the many roadblocks? How do they—and how do we—define success? Do influencers wake up one morning and suddenly label themselves successful and, more importantly, on that morning, do they suddenly realize lifelong fulfillment?

We examine such careers because time and again the psychological effects of influencers' lifestyles have proven dangerous. Michael Jackson succumbed to drug addiction. Ernest Hemingway suffered from depression and killed himself. O. J. Simpson went to jail, eventually. These celebrities were powerful market influencers during the height of their careers, yet they collapsed from the intense pressure and unrealistic expectations that public figures face from themselves and their followers. Unfortunately, these stories are prevalent in careers where a person becomes a commodity. Influencers may realize success by societal standards, but do they realize it by their own?

To make matters worse, influencers tend to judge their own careers based on their peers' successes. Studies have shown that people who spend more time on social media tend to be more depressed because they feel their lives are subpar to those of their friends and family. This is because their friends and family only post the best photos of their beach vacations, with perfect lighting and Photoshop editing that emulates a magazine cover. They don't share the rainy day, the eight hours of travel, or the icky hotel breakfast.

I hate to break it to you, but celebrities have been doing this for years. Famous rappers rented homes and cars to appear on *MTV Cribs*. Models' flaws are airbrushed. *The New York Times* best-seller list is not an accurate depiction of sales, as all retailers are not included in the data. The Harry Winston diamonds you see on the red carpet are only on loan. For the consumer, this is harmless hype. However, for influencers, who are competing instead of consuming, these falsities damage egos and confidence levels. They witness their peers' successes and wonder why they haven't achieved the same. Then they begin making hasty reactionary business decisions that could harm their long-term growth.

I once had to talk an artist out of a blind rage because her competitor landed a massive sponsorship. Why hadn't she gotten the sponsorship? Was there something wrong with her or her business? Did we, as her team, fail her? Nope. This artist only saw the ad that hit social media, but, like the rest of the consumers, what she couldn't see was that her competitor's father worked for the sponsoring company, and there was no money exchanged. There was absolutely nothing about that sponsorship that should have had any negative psychological effect on my artist, but it hit her ego hard for days and made her second-guess many strategies we had in place.

Isolation is another troubling trend we see from influencers in need of a robust and honest support system. I had the privilege of witnessing a Q&A session with psychologist and researcher Shawn Achor for Southern Methodist University's Tate Lecture Series in 2018, and he mentioned that the number one greatest predictor of long-term happiness is social connection. Yet, in my experience, the first thing an influencer does as they become more popular is shrink their circle of friends and family. Celebrities feel by doing so they are protecting themselves, when in actuality, they are setting themselves up for isolated misery. By disconnecting, the influencer ends up being surrounded with yes people and develops a dangerous and warped worldview.

To combat these types of issues, we turn to the teachings of positive psychology, a relatively new area of scientific study pioneered by Dr. Martin Seligman. Positive psychology focuses on how humans thrive. Most psychological studies aim to understand how to give a person relief from a mental ailment like PTSD or postpartum depression, but these scientists are discovering how the brain performs when there is no disorder. These pioneers are teaching others how to achieve overall well-being, operate at peak performance, and thrive.

Terms like *happiness, optimism, self-esteem, resilience, mindfulness, perseverance,* and *grit* are the focus of positive psychology. As this field of study becomes especially important to those who embark on the quest for success, these topics are monumental. An influencer who incorporates positive psychology into their daily life is highly likely to gain focus and energy, realize happiness, and stave off self-sabotage.

Positive psychology is vital to the business of influencers, but more important, to their mental health. The correlation between the two becomes reciprocal for influencers as personal lives become public lives and vice versa. Without a healthy psychological state, the business will fail. Without a healthy business, the psychological state will suffer. Influencers must find a fluid dance between the two.

REMOVING THE GOALPOST

Every semester I share one of the most popular TED Talks of all time with my music business students. In it, Shawn Achor, a faithful disciple of Dr. Seligman, shares his life lessons from his time at Harvard University, first as a student, then as a teacher's assistant. He notes that new students on campus arrived full of excitement and appreciation for the privilege that came with acceptance into the esteemed Harvard community. But, after just a few short weeks, he noticed most students' attitudes transformed, and many became stressed and depressed. The problem is, after the initial success of making it into Harvard, the students were immediately looking toward the next goal of making good grades. The short-term happiness they experienced upon reaching the initial goal and getting into Harvard quickly faded as the brain looked ahead to the next goal. This mentality becomes an endless quest if you are not cued in. Achor shares his findings:

> "Every time your brain has a success, you just changed the goalpost of what success looked like. You got good grades, now you have to get better grades, you got into a good school and after you get into a better one, you got a good job, now you have to get a better job, you hit your sales target, we're going to change it. **And if happiness is on the opposite side of success, your brain never gets there.**"

This is one of the most important findings from positive psychology research. It doesn't matter how big the achieved goal is; if a person is constantly looking down the road to the next milestone, they can never be satisfied. I share this research with my students to help combat negative psychological damage that occurs all too often with influencers. And, if this research had been released before I sat on that bus in Chicago years ago, I would have shared it with my artist.

He could not fully appreciate the level of success he had achieved because he was already so far from where he began. He no longer had the perspective of comparison to other artists who were still struggling to get past the same hurdles he had already leaped beyond. This artist had a major record label contract, which alone is a major feat. He had his own tour bus, which many major label artists cannot afford. He had multiple gold-selling singles, which means he sold 500,000 copies of each, and yet he still couldn't appreciate what he had accomplished because he was already looking toward the next hurdle.

This artist did in fact garner his first number one single on the radio chart for that song he was worrying over, and he has seen the top of the charts several more times since. He is now selling out shows across the country and has become a platinum-selling artist, having sold 1,000,000 copies of each album. I can almost guarantee, however, that he, and others like him, is still not satisfied because of the never-ending moving goalpost. So, my concern remains: When will he wake up fulfilled?

Will it be the day after he wins a Grammy? Or will it be the day after a Super Bowl halftime show? Do we rescind the word success from his byline if neither event occurs? Or here's a potentially worse scenario: What is the psychological response if one of these events does occur? I mean, what's bigger than the Super Bowl? For a performer, or athlete for that matter, to wake up the morning after the Super Bowl and feel there is nothing left to strive for is tragic. This predicament is the reason so many celebrities, and, apparently, Harvard students, slip into depression.

YOUR DEFINITION OF SUCCESS

The first thing an influencer must do to help combat self-sabotage is define success for himself or herself early on. Knowing their personalized definition of success is the only way to remove the ever-changing goalpost. When an artist asks where they should start building their career, my response is always, "I cannot tell you where to begin until you tell me where you want to end up."

Every career is different, every timeline unique. Specific advice I would give to one client would not be sufficient for the next, because what makes one happy or fulfilled cannot be duplicated. Building the underlying foundation that makes an influencer feel successful is his or her own responsibility. Why? Because every day an influencer is faced with multiple decisions that could lead them down different paths, and knowing the desired ending will help them dictate which fork in the road to take. The clearer their personalized definition of success is, the better odds they have of reaching their happy ending.

Put twenty people in a room and ask them to write down their definitions of success. The responses will be wildly different based on their personal experiences and perceptions of the world. Now, imagine those people are your employees, and you have asked them to define success for your career instead of their own. This exercise could put the entire team of dedicated workers at odds. Each person's advice will vary, founded on his or her own preconceived notions of success, thereby throwing the long-term business plan off course.

Successful influencers steer the team to their definition of success order to ensure focus and increase the odds of happiness.

A novice musician should ask whether they would feel more successful winning a Grammy or playing to a sold-out stadium. Does the passion for creating music come from hearing their song on the radio or does it come from singing songs for an energetic and adoring audience under a bright spotlight? The career paths to each of these different outcomes diverge at every step. That's important information for someone building an empire. It means that an influencer must maintain focus on their long-term goals every step of the way. Trying to attack everything at once will likely end in failure all around.

For instance, one artist I worked with identifies as a songwriter who prides himself on writing the best lyrically solid songs. He idolizes clever writers and constantly overanalyzes the real-life characters he meets. He's a born observer. Another artist walks offstage every night and mentally replays every note, breaks down every move, and hears again every sign of approval or disapproval from the crowd. He studies other performers like athletes study game tapes, and in this way he pursues performance perfection. A third artist I know would be perfectly happy experimenting on a recording studio console to exhaustion, testing new techniques and the physics of sound. He's a bona fide Sir George Martin and Brian Wilson rolled into one.

These artists are all amazing vocalists and present their music beautifully, but each brings an individualized, deeply rooted passion to their work. I collaborated with the first artist to make sure he wrote with as many other songwriters as possible. The varied perspectives from each writer led the artist down a path of exploration and creativity, fueling his passion and his technique. Once he built up an acceptable catalog of songs, we were able to secure a publishing deal. This publishing deal

salary that the artist was able to live on, as well as a team
lp promote his music to future industry supporters. This
ɔundation had to be in place before he could focus on
touring or recording. In fact, we pulled him off the road for a year so
that this plan could be accomplished.

In his future career, he could be signed to a major label, go on
tour with his idols, and possibly even gain millions of followers. You
know what else could happen? He could lose that record deal and
stop touring due to the lack of followers. No matter what happens in
his career, by laying the foundation in songwriting, he will always be
able to earn money doing what he is most passionate about and may
even rack up a few Grammy Awards along the way. His personalized
definition of success lives and dies by whether he can be a professional
songwriter, not a recording artist.

The second artist, who pursues performance perfection, did not
focus on songwriting. Instead, he played as many shows as possible
in as many dive bars and coffee shops as would have him. Every new
location presented its own live-production challenges, which he learned
to manipulate and work through. He touched fans on a physical level
and developed a strong following that launched him to larger and larger
venues. This artist could, and still does, perform songs written by other
songwriters, so there was no need to address a publishing income stream
until he'd aced the performance skills, which were the foundation of his
business. He has since played for hundreds of thousands of fans across
the world, sold millions of albums, and every now and then he'll write
a song that makes it to number one.

What about the third artist, the tech head? He set up a cot in a
recording studio and moved in. He invented a new and fresh sound
that hadn't been heard before by becoming engrossed in the world

of constantly changing recording technology. This allowed him to produce projects for other artists while taking the time to discover the music he wanted to create. Like the others, by concentrating on one area of his career, he was able to secure a source of income as he embarked on 10,000 hours of practice. By developing a personalized definition of success, these influencers were able to lay a foundation for their business, navigate their careers, and realize happiness along the way.

STRENGTHS THAT SHINE

I'm sure you've heard the phrase: Play to your strengths. In the business world, it is essential to know a company's strengths (S) and weaknesses (W) and opportunities (O) and threats (T) in order to prevent loss of income and increase the return on investment. The same holds true for influencers, yet I have never seen an influencer build out a SWOT analysis.

Discovering your strengths will be necessary to solidify aspects of your brand. What do you do better than your competition? What matrix of traits makes you unique? To answer these and to prepare for upcoming chapters, head over to my website (laurabull.com) and find the All Access section. Use the password "clover" to gain access to helpful tools, links, and every exercise in this book in an easily printable format. There you will find the link for Martin Seligman's University of Pennsylvania VIA Survey of Character Strengths test. The survey is free in the name of higher learning, so just register and print off your top five strengths. Take the time to review this information and contemplate how these traits show up in various areas of your life. Although we will not complete a full SWOT analysis together, I suggest you generate one to arm yourself with the knowledge. I provide a helpful printout regarding SWOT on my website to help get you started.

In the interest of your education, I will bare my soul and share how I fared on the character assessment. Of course, I'm not truly concerned with this news getting out, since the goal is to find everything I'm naturally great at. Of twenty-four possible strengths, the automatic test results prioritized my top five:

Strength #1

Industry, diligence, and perseverance—

You work hard to finish what you start. No matter the project, you "get it out the door" in timely fashion. You do not get distracted when you work, and you take satisfaction in completing tasks.

Strength #2

Honesty, authenticity, and genuineness—

You are an honest person, not only by speaking the truth, but by living your life in a genuine and authentic way. You are down-to-earth and without pretense; you are a "real" person.

Strength #3

Humor and playfulness—

You like to laugh and tease. Bringing smiles to other people is important to you. You try to see the light side of all situations.

Strength #4

Curiosity and interest in the world—

You are curious about everything. You are always asking questions, and you find all subjects and topics fascinating.

You like exploration and discovery.

Strength #5

Bravery and valor—

You are a courageous person who does not shrink from threat, challenge, difficulty, or pain. You speak up for what is right even if there is opposition. You act on your convictions.

These five strengths show up in everything I do and everything I am. If I take one aspect of my life—the writing of this book, for instance—all my strengths are woven into the binding. Yes, it has taken years to pull this book together, but ever since the idea fluttered into my consciousness, I knew it would have to come to fruition. I've done the research, pulled together my resources, and spent countless days and weeks writing.

Life has jumped in the way like a deer in front of a speeding car. I've moved to a new city, become engaged, got hitched, and had a baby, but I continue writing. Inch by inch, the Word document has grown and my thoughts have become more organized. In the near future, we will come to a speck somewhere on the space-time continuum where you are reading this.

A continued effort to do or achieve something despite difficulties, failure, or opposition is the definition of perseverance, my #1 strength. How do my other strengths factor into the writing of this book? I hope, as you flip through the pages, you witness the honesty and humor in my experiences relayed by my writing. That covers #2 and #3. What about #4? If I didn't have a natural tendency for curiosity, I would have been content with focusing only on my marketing projects, never thinking about all the other influencers out there who are struggling with brand identity. I never would have dived further into the research or discovered there may be a need for this information. Number 5 is valor. I'd say writing a book and putting it out into the world, aiming to help readers in a positive way, is brave. Just as a playwright sits nervously in the audience on opening night, I, too, will be praying that something that I've shared and labored over will strike a nerve with the audience.

How do your strengths play into your work? Do you recognize these characteristics in tasks or projects? Do they appear in your personal and public life? Once you've reviewed these strengths and the role they play in your personal life, you will learn how to effectively accentuate those characteristics in your business. Emphasizing positive traits and using them in a marketing campaign is an obvious tactic, but how are those qualities best presented to the consumer? Which ones are most effective for each specific brand? These are the questions that must be asked to develop an influencer brand.

One slight caveat before moving on: Be aware that these strengths may also give you trouble at times. For instance, I'm overly honest, which can come across as brutally harsh in certain situations. I have found myself in hot water on more than a few occasions, especially in a boardroom setting. I have also been known to use humor during inappropriate moments. Learn from the situations, move on, and remember why these traits make you shine 99 percent of the time.

TRUE GRIT

In middle school, between awkward cafeteria socializing and *My So-Called Life* episodes, I was a proud member of our school's choir. Singing was the one thing I excelled at, and therefore enjoyed. Each year, students from all over the area auditioned for the Texas Music Educators Association's All-Region Choir, which was a feeder choir to the All-State Choir. To make the cut for this regional choir was like a varsity football player making the state playoffs. In a state as large as Texas, the competition is fierce. Some schools were awarded only one or two slots for students; some schools, none.

With my choir director's encouragement, I found myself auditioning for, and winning, a spot in the choir during my seventh-grade year. I spent many hours working on the required materials during after-school sessions, and even though my jitters were high, I pulled through to victory followed by a shower of praise.

"You are such a talented young lady."

"You have such a beautiful voice."

Nice sentiments indeed, but the next year's audition was not so kind. In fact, it was a miserable failure. Although everyone claimed I had talent, the judges ruled that I did not. Or did they? The truth is, I hadn't seen the need to practice. Forget 10,000 hours. I didn't even practice for ten. I showed up woefully unprepared and was rewarded with a low ranking. *Why did I need to practice if I had the talent?* The reality is that those judges were evaluating my skill level, not my talent, and my adolescent self could not distinguish between the two. Of course, I practiced the following year and rejoined the choir, but I didn't grasp the dichotomy until years later.

Angela Duckworth, another Seligman disciple, stumbled across the disparities between talent and skill during her early workings with low-income children, which led to her lifelong research of grit. She found that some students who had talent in math did not manage good grades, yet some who struggled with numbers earned solid As. When she examined her students' behavior further, she discovered that talent or a high IQ does not equal success. Instead, she found a higher correlation for success in those who are gritty. So, she set out to research and measure grit in highly successful individuals.

Like Malcolm Gladwell before her, Duckworth first emphasizes effort over talent. She presents two equations that explain how one may get from talent to success:

$$\text{Talent} \times \text{Effort} = \text{Skill}$$
$$\text{Skill} \times \text{Effort} = \text{Achievement}$$

Notice that effort shows up twice on the path to achievement. Her point is that hard work and daily struggles are more important than talent. Everyone has to put in the effort, and the ones who put in the most are the ones who succeed.

Duckworth then redefined grit. After decades of analyzing data from former students to Navy SEALs, she has demonstrated that **true grit is the result of both passion and perseverance**: To be gritty, one must have a deep love for what they do and the willingness to muddle through the hard stuff just to be able to do it, regardless of the outcome. Would you be willing to embark on a career, knowing that it could take twenty years before you saw any awards, accolades, or a sizable stash of cash? Would you still love what you do, even if those rewards did not come to fruition? If the answer to these questions is yes, then you have found your grit.

One of my friends in the industry who lives on the road (a difficult life by any measure) reminds himself on the bad days: My job is better than your vacation. He so deeply loves what he does, day in and day out, that when the bus breaks down on the side of the road, he still pushes ahead to the next day. He doesn't make a lot of money, he's away from his family 200 days a year, and he has no job security, but he's out there living his best life. He loves every second. This mentality sums up how passionate and persistent a person has to be to achieve their personalized definition of success.

How gritty do you think you are? Let's find out! Go over to my website (laurabull.com) and find the Grit Survey with your All Access pass. This tool, created by Duckworth and her colleagues, will measure your grit level. In just ten easy questions, the University of Pennsylvania will spit out a score between 1 and 5 (5 being the grittiest) and a graph that illustrates where that score fits with others who have been polled. I was not surprised to learn my grit level was a 4.58, placing me higher than 93 percent of respondents my age.

The artist on that tour bus in Chicago lost his grit for a minute when he lost sight of his personalized definition of success. The goalpost right in front of him (reaching the top of the radio chart) turned his focus away from his passion and shackled his perseverance. He momentarily lost confidence, perspective, passion, and control over his own destiny, but a little reminder of his unique definition of success brought it all back into focus.

If you've been paying attention to successful influencers and how they got there, you've probably heard the term grit many times. You already know that, to get there yourself, you will need all the grit you can muster. If you scored low, don't fret. After losing her husband suddenly in 2015, Facebook's COO Sheryl Sandberg wrote about building resilience in her book *Option B: Facing Adversity, Building Resilience, and Finding Joy*. She believes that anyone can develop grit in three steps: Discover what you are passionate about, practice, and find your purpose by believing your work matters to others. You'll read more about that coming up.

WHAT'S NEXT?

No matter which industry you choose, knowing your strengths and weaknesses, your grit and perseverance levels, and your personalized definition of success will help you determine your path to achievement. With this knowledge, you will have the ammunition you need to bulldoze any roadblocks along the way and combat self-sabotage. Remember to do the following before proceeding to Chapter 4:

- Identify your strengths.
- Identify your passion and level of grit.
- Define your personalized version of success, your ultimate goal. Write it out. This is just a hypothesis for now, as we are about to dig into your purpose.
- Practice, practice, practice! Start working on your 10,000 hours!

TIP: Get yourself a Panda Planner (pandaplanner.com). By utilizing positive psychology principles on a daily basis, you increase productivity, heighten creativity, and ensure that you enjoy each yard gained on your way to the ultimate goalpost.

— 4 —

THE FIVE PS OF

SUCCESSFUL INFLUENCERS

••••

*"Ultimately, we all have to decide for ourselves what
constitutes failure, but the world is quite eager to give
you a set of criteria if you let it. So I think it fair to say
that by any conventional measure, a mere seven years
after my graduation day, I had failed on an epic scale.
An exceptionally short-lived marriage had imploded, and
I was jobless, a lone parent, and as poor as it is possible
to be in modern Britain without being homeless. The
fears that my parents had had for me, and that I had
had for myself, had both come to pass, and by every usual
standard, I was the biggest failure I knew."*

—J. K. Rowling, self-made billionaire and best-selling
author, Harvard commencement speech, 2008

••••

The fact that Harry Potter began his existence as an idea on a
train is fitting: His adolescent adventures took off around the
world at runaway speed with J. K. Rowling as his engineer and with

millions of kids and adults along for the ride. The electric world of Harry Potter lives on the pages of over 500 million books worldwide, in blockbuster films, in dedicated amusement parks, and even on the stage. He is the most recognizable wizard in the world and has become the most sold book series in history. Maybe more surprising, he became the catalyst for one down-on-her-luck single mother to become one of the world's most successful authors.

J. K. Rowling's is the epitome of a rags-to-riches story; some say she's richer than the queen of England. And although that's where most of the media tend to focus, the real headline lies in her transformation into an influencer. News flash: That transformation had nothing to do with her net worth or lack thereof. Within the lines of her Harvard commencement speech, which has been viewed millions of times and even published, she allows a small glimpse into her innate disposition. Here one may discover the features of her character that ultimately propelled her into the stratosphere.

In my experience with a large number of thriving influencers, Rowling's character and outlook are not unique. These commonalities can be narrowed to five key foundations.

THE 5 PS OF THRIVING INFLUENCERS

Passion
An intense desire or enthusiasm for something

Perseverance
The ability to be steadfast in reaching long-term goals despite difficulties

Positivity
The ability to assess situations truthfully while
maintaining a positive outlook

Purpose
A worthy and valid reason for one's endeavors that
ultimately helps others beyond oneself

Power
Acknowledging, conserving, and harnessing one's
power over their own destiny

The most important aspect of these foundational elements is that they are all interconnected. Passion and purpose create power and positivity. Positivity generates perseverance and power. Power aids purpose, and so on. They multiply their individual and combined strength exponentially by feeding off one another.

Passion and perseverance, as discussed in the last chapter, are the foundational elements of grit. That gritty nature overflows in Rowling. She defied her parents in order to explore her passion for writing, despite knowing what it could cost her. It seemed clear to the idealistic college student that she must be passionate about what she did for a living in order to maintain an adequate level of overall well-being, regardless of an empty bank account and unhappy family gatherings.

As we dissect the remaining three aspects of a thriving influencer— positivity, power, and purpose—notice how Rowling had to embrace more than just passion and perseverance to reach billionaire status.

Just like her main character, she has become a beacon of positivity and power. With that power, she fulfilled her true purpose, not as a writer, but as an advocate for those less fortunate.

PURPOSE

You are standing on the roof of a high-rise looking several stories down. There is a solid wooden plank leading to the adjacent roof about twenty feet away. You notice a large suitcase on the other side. That suitcase contains $5 million. No one else is around, so if you can get to it, you keep it. Would you attempt to cross? Maybe.

Now imagine that this particular afternoon is windy, and foggy. The plank is only twelve inches wide, but sturdy. And, in the interest of full disclosure, I must inform you that only 80 percent of those who have attempted to cross it have succeeded. That doesn't sound too bad, does it? Okay, maybe it does.

What if I offered more money? Five million dollars doesn't seem like much these days, so let's make it $50 million. Remember, there is a 20 percent chance you could fall to your death, but hey, if you make it you are an instant millionaire. Would you take the chance?

Performance coach and psychologist Jim Loehr poses this hypothetical scenario when lecturing on how internal narratives affect the quest for success. In a roomful of people, most would not accept such a daunting challenge, even for $50 million. I would be tempted just for the sake of competition but wouldn't follow through. However, when he replaces the prize money with something that most find essential, everyone accepts. Instead of $50 million, the subject must cross the plank to save their immediate family from death. With this new development, is there even a choice? The reward matters. Embarking on a worthy cause to help someone else is an example of purpose.

Psychological clarity is as important to an athlete's training regimen as the physical, if not more so. What creates the drive to push past pain and grueling schedules? What makes someone spend their entire life striving to reach a goal, ignoring the possibility that the goal could be unattainable? What allows someone to turn a blind eye to extreme competition or negative commentators? A person who merely wants to be successful for the sake of success will likely fall short during these relentless hardships. A person who is grounded in purpose, however, will likely continue to strive toward the seemingly impossible goal.

Purpose is the conviction that your work matters, that you are helping others in some way. I stumbled upon mine in my early twenties at Sony Music Nashville. A few years into my tenure, our new president called us to the conference room to introduce himself. His words were powerful enough to stay with me for almost two decades now.

First and foremost, he said he always had been and always would be a fan of the music that comes out of Music City. He wanted us to appreciate how passionate he was about what we all did for a living and to understand why he had worked so hard and for so long. His openness and likability bonded everyone in that room to him. He then mentioned that every day he woke up, looked into the mirror, and asked the same question: Am I making someone's dream come true? Should the day arrive when he answered no, he said he would leave the music industry forever.

His passion was music; his purpose was making dreams come true. He went to the office every day, dealt with compliance issues and budget cuts, staff layoffs and contractual obligations, all to make someone's dream come true. But the day-to-day job was just his vehicle to accomplish his true purpose.

> Passion ≠ Purpose
>
> but
>
> Passion + Purpose = Perseverance

Most people mistakenly interchange purpose and passion. Unfortunately, it is possible to have one without the other.

The goal is to develop passion for a purpose because in doing so, you instinctively develop perseverance.

The psychologist Angela Duckworth agrees with Loehr that purpose is at the root of a person's drive, the root of a life's mission statement. One has to really want to practice in order to be better, to obsess over a goal in order to be the best. Ultimately, achieving purpose leads to fulfillment.

My boss's speech made me see my own purpose. Many jobs could serve as the conduit to achieving the same purpose. It might sound glamorous, but the reality of a lowly record label employee is not ideal. With sixty-hour workweeks, no benefits, and no recognition, I would have made more money with fewer headaches if I had chosen to continue waiting tables at TGI Fridays. Yet, instinctively I understood delivering Ultimate Margaritas was not fulfilling my purpose. From helping artists live up to their full potential, to releasing projects into the marketplace, to teaching students how to enter a demanding career with the tools necessary to succeed, my goal is to help them all win. If my epitaph reads, "she made dreams come true," I'll be happy from the other side.

I was working with a female duo act that had been struggling for years to break into the national country music scene. They had achieved mild regional success and were seeking out remedies for their lackluster brand. Some on their team thought it may be a styling issue; some thought the product was weak compared to the competition. As I do with all of my clients, I walked them through a story-prompting exercise that is designed to make sure an authentic message and a greater purpose is revealed. What they discovered changed the course of their career.

You see, one of these young ladies survived a brain tumor. As a result, she was an advocate of a healthy lifestyle and she had a strong desire to give back to young cancer patients. Once she was able to take a closer look at her true purpose, she decided to alter her course. She went from struggling to achieve success in country music to developing a children's musical act. She and her twin sister now produce children's albums, perform at family-friendly festivals and charity events, and maintain a healthy lifestyle as a positive example for their young audience.

Once their purpose came into focus, their goals and actions changed; once their actions changed, the brand became unique and authentic.

An influencer must define this individualized purpose as they aim to establish a mission statement for their brand. To develop a strong sense of self that can be relayed to the general public without a well-defined core purpose is an impossible feat. When I ask an influencer why they do what they do, they should respond with purpose, not passion: "I'm doing this job to take care of my family. I'm doing this job to help domestic violence become a national conversation. I'm doing this job because I want to make someone forget about their shitty day for just a few minutes." These are all purpose statements.

On the other hand, these are passion statements: "I love to sing. I like to entertain people. I live for fashion. I love making money." An influencer with passion-driven responses is not going to make it very far. They will not stand apart from the competition or develop a shared identity with the audience. And what's worse, they will not be able to muster grit when the going gets tough, because a person who doesn't stand for anything will be pliable to outside forces, of which there are many.

Investors and fans alike look for rich history and meaning. They look for someone who has conviction born of introspection. They look for someone who can give them a glimpse into their purpose so that they can connect and relate.

J. K. Rowling has a passion for writing, but her purpose is much deeper. Before Potter was even a dream, her work at Amnesty International began her lifetime of dedication to human rights worldwide. Her current world stage has allowed her to be an outspoken activist for women and the LGBTQ community, reaching millions of followers with just one tweet. And she is a fierce advocate for the impoverished, the souls whose fate she once shared before Harry Potter. Just as she wrote of her protagonist, her purpose is to help people overcome adversity and instill hope. To see Rowling's purpose, you need only pick up a book.

POSITIVITY

In addition to purpose, influencers often overlook the power of positivity. Society as a whole tends to downplay psychological ailments, let alone acknowledge the very real influence that a thriving human psyche can play on a successful career. Words like *happiness, well-being, optimism,* and *grit* are often seen as superficial. Yet, thanks to positive psychologists like Seligman, Duckworth, and Achor, among many others, there is now clear scientific data to prove the impact that happiness plays in professional and private lives. During Achor's TED Talk he shares the following statistics:

"If you can raise somebody's level of positivity in the present, then their brain experiences what we now call a happiness advantage, which is, your brain at positive performs significantly better than at negative, neutral, or stressed. Your intelligence rises, your creativity rises, your energy levels rise. In fact, we've found that every single business outcome improves. Your brain at positive is 31 percent more productive than your brain at negative, neutral, or stressed. You're 37 percent better at sales. Doctors are 19 percent faster—more accurate at coming up with the correct diagnosis when positive instead of negative, neutral, or stressed."

That's right! Influencers can actually increase their creativity and clarity if they consciously maintain positivity, so why isn't this the very first thing on everyone's to-do list?

Positivity can be the slight edge needed to go from average to outlier.

The life of an influencer, however, can be anything but positive. Constant external negativity by way of social media, reviews, and numerous stressors leads to internal negativity. Some are prone to pessimism to begin with, giving a false perception of reality. Instead of combating this negativity with positive thoughts, some influencers tend to withdraw from society and begin self-medicating with drugs, alcohol, and other self-destructive habits that alleviate their distress. Witnessing an influencer cycling down a self-fulfilling prophecy of failure due to a faulty perception of their world is downright tragic. Even those who have achieved high levels of public success are not immune: Elvis Presley, Marilyn Monroe,

Prince, Michael Jackson, Robin Williams, Philip Seymour Hoffman, River Phoenix, Heath Ledger, Kurt Cobain, Alexander McQueen, Ernest Hemingway, Vincent van Gogh, John Belushi, Chris Farley. The only way to combat internal strife is to learn how to rewrite the internal narrative— the story we tell ourselves. And as Jim Loehr says,

"The most important story you will ever tell about yourself is the story you tell to yourself."

Loehr teaches his clients how to reprogram their internal narratives in order to transform their business and personal lives. With purpose at the epicenter, he is able to give Olympians the psychological edge that pushes them into the winner's circle by making them just two seconds faster. Internal narratives are so important that they are the difference between winning and losing.

Loehr ascertains that faulty assumptions are a major disruption to internal narratives, and yet most people are unaware of how prevalent these false assumptions are in their daily lives. Some narratives inside our heads are harmless: "That restaurant is going to be so crowded at this time of day," or "I'm sure the tickets are already all gone." Some are less harmless: "I forgot to bring money for the school fund-raiser, and the other parents are going to think I'm just awful." Others are downright detrimental: "I lost my record deal because I'm not good enough. The fans must not like me. I'll never be able to earn a living doing what I love." That's quite a leap in reasoning. Where's the proof to back any of this up? Do we know that's why the record contract ended?

When an artist loses their record deal, nine times out of ten, it has nothing to do with how talented or wonderful that person is. External factors are most likely the culprit: A label could be struggling with budget cuts, or the trends in the marketplace could be shifting, or their manager could be difficult to deal with. Actually, the latter is often the reason, but I digress. The point is that an artist can still have a career, sometimes a better career, even after the loss of a record deal. In fact, most artists go through their careers with multiple record contracts. Even Dolly Parton, the queen of Nashville, has made the rounds at the major labels like Sony, Warner, and Universal, and many of the independent labels as well.

Just like our imaginary artist, a pessimistic person believes that if something bad happens to them, they are at fault. They were too stupid to get a good grade, the competition was better, and they were unlucky again. This thinking leads to self-sabotage and, as Sheryl Sandberg and Adam Grant mention in *Option B*, the "primary loss leads to secondary losses." The initial loss of a record deal leads to secondary losses of confidence, loss of self-awareness, and the loss of so many other traits that are necessary to becoming a powerful influencer.

An optimistic person, however, believes that if they encounter a negative situation, it was caused by external factors and therefore they are able to maintain the hope of future prospects. This mentality allows for a quicker recovery and the ability to see other possibilities clearly. The optimistic artist loses their record deal and decides to use that as an opportunity. They have the confidence to find another record deal or find another way to fulfill their purpose, like writing songs for other artists, which is oftentimes more lucrative.

Blind optimism, however, is also a danger. An optimist could view himself or herself as indestructible and impervious to factors that could hinder their long-term goals. They could potentially miss vital warning signs that could impact their business, because they are blinded by their inability to be objective. An influencer must rely on facts to rewrite their internal narratives by doing the following:

1. Recognize that negative self-talk may be based on faulty assumptions. Stop and ask yourself if your conclusions are based on facts.

2. Decipher the facts that may alter your perception of the situation. Seek out the truth of the matter.

The influencer that makes faulty assumptions about how and why a setback occurred is the one who gets lost in pessimism and subsequently gets lost in their career. The influencer who seeks out the truth of the situation, however, is the influencer who regains positivity and control.

Self-awareness and self-efficacy lead to confidence, power, and optimism, all of which are necessary to be successful influencers.

Imagine if a young J. K. Rowling, a single mother drowning in poverty, had allowed faulty assumptions about her reality to cloud her judgment. She might not have been happy, but she remained optimistic and hopeful, or she wouldn't have soldiered on. What if she had assumed her skill level wasn't high enough after receiving her first rejection letter? Could she have seen this as a challenge? What if she had assumed no one wanted to read an adolescent story about an orphaned wizard battling an all-powerful sorcerer? The answer is simple: There would be no Harry Potter.

POWER

Choosing the life of an influencer is tantamount to choosing adversity. There will be many, many times that the public will attack on what seems to be a personal level. There will also be many times that external factors will affect your life and career. But, to brave souls everywhere, I come bearing good news. You, and only you, have complete power over your destiny, and that knowledge alone will give you a sense of empowerment. Remember, an influencer who has power is able to acknowledge, conserve, and harness their power over their own destiny.

In *Option B*, Sandberg and Grant share the results of a classic behavioral experiment on stress. The participants in the study had to concentrate on a task while bombarded by loud noises, which, of course, caused high levels of stress and frustration. As a reprieve, certain subjects were given a button that would stop the noises. It is no surprise that these participants showed greater concentration and reduced anxiety. The interesting twist, however, is that "*none of the participants actually pressed the button.* Stopping the noise didn't make the difference . . . Knowing they *could* stop the noise did. The button gave them a sense of control and allowed them to endure the stress."

This demonstrates that even the illusion of control provides the mental capacity necessary to remain positive and steadfast in the face of hardship. The difference between feeling in control and not is the difference between success and failure. Influencers, therefore, must learn how to focus their energy on the situations they can control, instead of wasting their energy on those they can't.

When my employer, Sony BMG Music Entertainment, started layoffs, I wasted valuable energy worrying about the unemployment line even though I had absolutely no power over this external crisis. My friends and I were numbers on a spreadsheet, and in the end I got to keep my job, but not because I was better than any one of them. The external world, or God, if one chooses to believe, would decide the outcome, but only I could determine my fate. I had to relinquish control over the situation and harness it elsewhere. Lose the battle, but win the war.

Realizing the lack of control in one situation allows a person to focus valuable energy on the areas of life they can control. I had no control over whether or not I was going to keep my job, but I did have control over how well I did my job, thereby creating the possibility of better opportunities elsewhere, regardless of the outcome. I wasted my energy trying to keep up with political games, when I should have been helping my artists succeed. Concentrating on creating a smarter, stronger, and more self-aware version of myself would have provided the positive energy needed to make it through a difficult time.

Jim Loehr shares this energy pyramid in his book *The Power of Story: Change Your Story, Change Your Destiny in Business and in Life.* Loehr believes humans have a finite amount of energy allotted to sustain life, and therefore, determining where that energy is expended maximizes human existence. He places physical energy, emotional energy, mental energy, and spiritual energy in a pyramid like Maslow's hierarchy of needs, with physical as an anchor and spiritual as the mast:

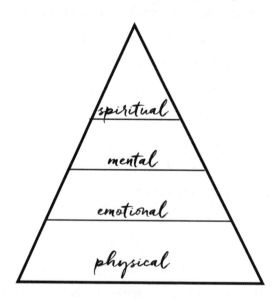

This pyramid visually showcases how influencers should conserve and employ energy in order to thrive.

Remember,

When an influencer is unhealthy, their company is unhealthy as well.

So, how does an influencer direct their energy in a positive way to succeed? The best way to stave off exhaustion and remain efficient is to take control by employing goals and subsequent action steps. Research has shown time and again that focusing on small goals and implementing new habits lead to a sense of accomplishment and reduced anxiety and depression. The mind is clearer and therefore capable of making better decisions.

Creating a list of short-term goals every few weeks and executing the correct and positive action steps that will help accomplish those goals will lead to success. Action steps may include baby steps. Start work at the same time every day, schedule regular meetings with members of the team, read an inspirational book once a month, spend at least one hour a day promoting your brand on social media. These are all good examples of short-term action steps that may turn into long-term habits. As the career progresses, those healthy habits will turn into accomplishments. Obviously, these generic actions should become more succinct as time goes on in order to conserve energy and harness power for the areas of business that matter.

In addition, an influencer needs to learn how to take control over the trajectory of their career and hold themselves accountable for the highs and lows. One of my artist friends had a manager who was two-faced, acting laid-back and friendly in front of him, but then in business meetings becoming downright rude and entitled. He even cussed out a marketing executive. This reflected poorly on my friend and he ended up losing his record deal.

The difficulty is that everyone in his circle, including myself, was afraid to tell him the truth about his trusted advisor. You see, a manager and an artist are sometimes so close they are like family, and telling one something negative about the other is like a best friend revealing a cheating husband. It never ends well for the messenger. Another real possibility was that the artist actually knew about, and potentially even directed, the poor behavior. Either way, no one wanted to be involved, and the artist suffered. He not only relinquished power, but he also did so to the wrong person.

The artist's responsibility is to direct his own career, to show up to those meetings, to maintain communication with the key people involved at his record label. He could have asked others what was happening, but his faulty assumptions about the situation clouded his perception of reality and he lost control over his destiny. A successful influencer doesn't whine and give up if things don't go their way. They expose problems and address them with realistic remedies. Only those that correct, or redirect, can survive as an influencer.

Unlike my friend, Rowling redirected her energy to concentrate on what she could control. She wrote her destiny instead of allowing her circumstances to do so. She was a penniless single mom, so she spent her time on the train to and from work to accomplish her goals. By harnessing her energy to create Harry Potter, she pulled herself and her daughter out of poverty. It took years of baby action steps to find her way onto bookstore shelves everywhere, but once there, her power as an influencer has continued to surpass even her own expectations.

WHAT'S NEXT?

Let's harness your five Ps!

- Sort your top ten priorities. These should be pulled from all areas of your life—social, occupational, and anything else requiring your time and dedication.
- Take that information and define your purpose. Write down what will be written on your epitaph.
- Acknowledge three substantial faulty assumptions you've had in the past regarding your career. How did they affect the outcome of those situations? Apply an optimistic lens to those moments and ask if the outcome could have been different.
- Write down five short-term goals. Now write down which daily action steps you will implement in order to create long-term habits that will further your career. Now go do it!

PART 2

The Brand Matrix

– 5 –

THE ORIGINATION OF
A BRAND

●●●●

FADE IN:

Tall grass blows at sunset, decorating the banks of a small pond. On a slight slope, a young girl in a pastel cotton sundress lies listening to an acoustic song on her transistor radio.

CUT TO:

Just a few miles away, a young boy's beat-up Chevy truck breaks down along a two-lane country road. In defeat, he turns on the radio. When he hears the country twang of Tim McGraw, he is immediately transported to an open field where he and the young girl frolic among the trees. Then they are in the back of his truck cuddling on a warm blanket gazing up at the bright stars. Then they are walking down a wooded trail holding hands with fireflies lighting their way.

CUT TO:

An old barn nearby provides the backdrop for this young girl and her acoustic guitar. She's playing a sweet love song to her high school crush . . .

And the girl next door is propelled to superstardom.

●●●●

In 2006, Taylor Swift released her first single, "Tim McGraw," to country radio. She was just seventeen years old. As we revisit her music video debut, the setting and script present a generic version of a standard country music song. Thousands of videos mimic the same themes. I should know. I'm responsible for at least 100 of them. So, how did this video with all the common elements stand out? How did Taylor rise above the rest of her competition? How was she able to grow from a teen country star to bona fide pop star when so many others have failed?

When you look at Taylor's musical journey over the past decade, this debut video couldn't be more authentic to her brand. I realize this may be a shocking statement based on her current musical offerings, which feature pop stars and rap artists, electric guitars and backup dancers, and designer clothes with blood-red lipstick. One YouTube comment recently posted beneath the "Tim McGraw" video simply states, "Hello, old Taylor." True, she is no longer a novice and her style has evolved considerably over the years, but the Taylor Swift brand has not changed.

When it comes to branding, there is a major difference between evolution and change.

To understand how Taylor has been able to stand the test of time and repeated pop-culture scandal, we must turn to the brand matrix: the point in which the brand originates. Imagine a Venn diagram where each of the three major components of a brand—the product, image, and narrative—are equally represented and balanced. Marketers must closely examine the various characteristics of an influencer, their lives and passions, personality traits and strengths, and then decipher the few key traits that intersect in the middle. Together these core pillars, where the three components coexist, create the brand matrix.

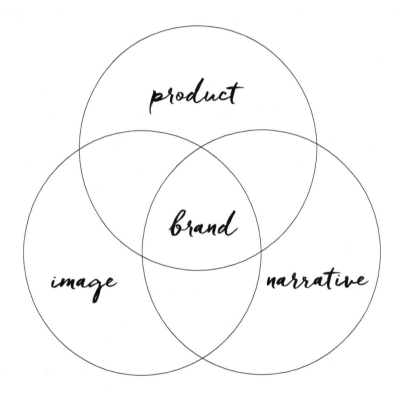

The **product** in the brand matrix is what is being sold to the consumer. When teaching this to my students, I replace the product that is a person with a product that is an item, like a perfume bottle, in order to make this concept easier to understand. The actual chemical composition of the perfume is the product. It's the aroma that is the only scent in the world like it. It might smell flowery yet modern, which is different from the bottle next to it that smells flowery yet vintage. It may be quite subtle, but there is something about it that makes it unique and more desirable over the others for a particular consumer.

The **image** in the brand matrix is the visual representation of a product. A perfume's packaging is the first representation of that product a consumer will see as it sits on the shelf among its peers. The appearance should evoke what that liquid inside the bottle is going to smell like and how it is different from all the others. Romance by Ralph Lauren is packaged in a solid, clear glass bottle with an elegant silver square cap inside a soft pink and metallic box. From the colors to the font to the crisp, clean lines, the packaging says this product is uncomplicated, delicate, feminine, and classy. The description online says the product "features notes of exhilarating florals, creamy woods, and seductive musk." The packaging and the bottle look flirtatious and romantic. They match the description of the scent.

In comparison, the classic men's cologne Polo by Ralph Lauren is bottled in a forest green glass flask with a gold cap resembling the tip of a polo stick. The bottle and box showcase a gold imprint of a polo player in mid-swing on a horse. The audience imagines a country club, where men are sipping brandy and smoking cigars. The same online store describes Polo as having a "masculine base note blend of leather, tobacco, cedar, balsam, patchouli, and oak moss." Again, the scent and the package are cohesive. If Polo smelled of dandelions on an ocean breeze, Ralph Lauren would have a serious branding problem.

The **narrative** in the brand matrix is the message of the product and the image. The narrative incites an emotional response to the product. For many brands, this narrative is in the form of catchy taglines like Just Do It. Nike sells shoes and athletic wear, but think back to their mission statement: "To bring inspiration and innovation to every athlete in the world." Their statement does not mention their products. Nike's stated purpose goes beyond selling shoes to make a profit. With Just Do It, Nike imbues the mission statement with emotion and inspires its customers to push past perceived limits and achieve physical feats like superstar athletes. It implies, if you wear Nike, you have the power to accomplish anything. That's a lot to say in just three words.

Though it sounds counterintuitive, the message, in the form of a tagline or creative ad copy, is not necessary to communicate a narrative. In many Ralph Lauren commercials, the audience is only shown images of couples frolicking about to the sounds of a seductive music bed. In fact, most perfume commercials are metaphorical, created to incite emotion. If a consumer reaction is achieved, the narrative is being communicated effectively with or without using dialogue.

Narratives must speak to the product's target audience and resonate with their beliefs in order to achieve a desired reaction, but they must also accurately portray the product and the image. These three components must come together, presenting a clear brand, or the consumer will become confused. When I hear the word Nike, the first thing that comes to mind is "Just Do It." One glimpse of the swoosh, and I either think of Nike or Just Do It, or both. Product, image, and narrative are interchangeable. Whenever the consumer encounters one component of a brand, they should think of the brand as a whole. That is the true test of a successful brand.

OH, KANYE!

Remember that time Kanye West interrupted Taylor Swift's MTV Video Music Awards acceptance speech by leaping onto the stage, yanking the mic mid-sentence, and proclaiming, "Yo Taylor, I'm really happy for you. I'ma let you finish, but Beyoncé has one of the best videos of all time!"

Gasp! Even Beyoncé cringed! Poor Taylor stood center stage, on live television, mute, shocked, and devastated as the camera made an awkward cut to the next segment. The incident is one of the more painful television moments of pop-culture history. And yet, it is possibly one of the best moments of Taylor's career.

These two polarized brands colliding onstage could have left career debris scattered about. Instead, the incident played perfectly to each entertainer's core audience, highlighted the important elements of each brand, and raised each artist's level of superstardom a notch. Kanye was rude and heartless; Taylor remained friendly and sympathetic. Kanye was kicked out of the award show; Taylor was seen backstage crying. Kanye was shunned by his fellow artists; Taylor received industry-wide support. Both saw an increase in record sales. How is this possible?

What is the first thing you think of when you hear the name Taylor Swift? When I pose this question during a word-association game, many of my students come up with the following:

> Songwriter, relationships, girl next door, girl squad, Kanye, pretty, blonde, relatable, country (depending on which side of the room they're on), pop (the other side of the room), rich, ambitious, red, breakups, strong, gossip, all-American.

Somewhere in the middle of that jumble is Taylor's brand.

Sure, all of these terms could be used to describe Taylor at any given point throughout her career, but which are the core elements that are constant? Where do these terms fall in the Venn diagram? Which ones share the sweet spot in the middle?

Note that in the music business, the product being sold is the music: the themes, the sound, and the tone. The product is the unique composition we hear on the radio. Which aspects of Taylor's songs have remained consistent from Old Taylor to Current Taylor? Look past the electric guitar and rap beats.

Let's do this together. Referring to my students' adjectives above, which could describe her product, image, and narrative?

PRODUCT	IMAGE	NARRATIVE
Songwriter	Songwriter	Songwriter
Relationships	Relationships	Relationships
Girl Next Door	Girl Next Door	Girl Next Door
Girl Squad	Girl Squad	Girl Squad
Relatable	Pretty	Relatable
Country/Pop	Blonde	Rich
Breakups	Relatable	Ambitious
Strong	Rich	Breakups
Gossip	Red	Strong
All-American	Breakups	Gossip
	All-American	All-American

Whew! We were able to use all of the terms except for Kanye. Even though there is a transference of awareness when someone thinks about the back-and-forth feuding between these two artists over time, Kanye has absolutely nothing to do with Taylor's core brand. He didn't build it and he isn't a part of it. He is a tangential story line.

Now, let's put the above attributes into the Venn diagram to easily visualize the core elements of her brand.

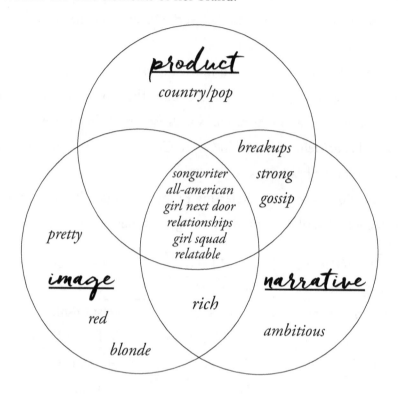

BRAND MATRIX = Songwriter, Relationships, Girl Next Door, Girl Squad, Relatable, All-American

Using this Venn diagram allows us to step back and see the various elements of the brand, how they play together, and which are the true foundations that should remain consistent over time. The traits that do not fall into the center are still part of the overall brand and are accurate statements about the singer, but these are expendable and changeable. She can dye her hair brown, she can lose her money, and she can start playing the drums and her audience will still show up to buy her products as long as the core elements do not change.

Now let's build Taylor's brand statement based on this diagram.

First, having everything laid out, we can cut redundancies: *all-American* goes hand in hand with *girl next door,* *girl squad* could be classified as part of her relationships. Which do we keep? Which are more accurate descriptions? More important, which will work better twenty years from now? For instance, *girl squad* is a fad term that will disappear before this book hits the shelves.

Next, this is the time to open a thesaurus and come up with the best vocabulary that can showcase her brand. Do we have the best terms already? I think we can do better than songwriter. Is Taylor a poet, a songsmith, or a lyricist? Yes, all of these could apply depending on your personal view, but none of these are the best options. *Storyteller,* on the other hand, is a pretty spot-on description of her music and will allow her the flexibility of evolution and experimentation. This term does not confine her in a specific genre. More important, it sets her apart from the competition.

Could there be a better term for *relatable?* This is a term that should describe all influencers, so we should dig deeper. How is she relatable? *Engaging* would accurately describe how she interacts with fans on and off stage, and it's a stronger action word, but it would be difficult to express this verb under the image and product components. Would *affable* describe her open and friendly relationship with her fans? How about the modest way she dresses, whether in sweatshirts and jeans, sundresses and cowgirl boots, or even fashionable bodysuits? All of these styles don't show too much skin, and all would be perfectly acceptable when meeting a significant other's parents for the first time. Does *affable* depict some of the themes of her music? I think so! It sounds counterintuitive, but the more specific the core pillars are now, the more opportunities for authentic growth later.

And, with that, we are now ready to write our brand statement: Taylor Swift is the affable and earnest girl next door who shares stories about her life and personal <u>relationships</u> through her music: she is a charming <u>storyteller</u>.

DISSECTING A BRAND

With the brand statement above, we utilized the shared perception of Taylor Swift in a rapid-fire brainstorming session among my students. Now we must confirm these core elements are woven deep into the fabric of her life and her brand before we make it official. Each carefully chosen word should be rich with meaning, including earnest, personal, and charming.

Taylor's brand must be generic enough to allow her artistic creativity to venture and evolve, but specific enough to separate her brand from the competition.

First, her music is notorious for offering sneak peeks into her personal life. Each lyric is like a diary entry shared with the world. She depicts her high school hallways, high-profile breakups, friendships, and even commentary on her critics' comments. At age fourteen, Swift was the youngest writer to sign a publishing deal with mega-publisher Sony/ATV Music Publishing, but as we determined, the term *songwriter* is too nebulous to accurately describe what Taylor does so well. A storyteller, on the other hand, recounts a narration with relatable emotion, and that is the core of her product.

The term *storyteller* supersedes a genre specification and allows her to maneuver easily between country and pop (pop just means popular, anyway). The storyteller moniker also allows her to write about her life as she matures, permitting her longtime audience to grow with her and even attracting new audiences along the way. This is the key to how she survived both a genre switch and evolving her brand into her twenties, beating the dreaded teenage icon death sentence.

Storyteller is a major characteristic of the product, but remember, to be considered a core element it must fit in with the other two components of the brand, image and narrative. The label *storyteller* fits nicely into the narrative of Taylor's brand. She is very open about pulling from real-life situations for her songwriting. Mainstream media even jokes that if anyone dates Taylor Swift, they have to know the details of the inevitable breakup are going to end up on the radio. In addition, she doesn't just write her own songs. She is vocal about writing songs for other artists and how cathartic the storytelling process is for her.

Now let's turn to the image component of Taylor's brand. Here we are looking for visual representations. Many of Taylor's music videos follow a clear storyline instead of abstract or metaphorical images, and her live performances do the same. Not only that, every time she shows up onstage with a fellow artist known for their songwriting abilities (Ed Sheeran, John Mayer) she reinforces this narrative through transference. Therefore, we do, in fact, see storytelling show up in product, image, and narrative. It's safe to say that term can now be considered a core element of the Taylor Swift brand.

Next, we look at the word *affable*. We use this term to illustrate how important it is to Taylor to maintain a personal connection with her fans. She does this through lyrics (product) and through social media (narrative). As a young artist, she practically created the world of online influencers when she utilized Myspace to interact with each follower. Today, her fans call themselves Swifties. She keeps up with them on her blog and personally leaves messages on their social media profiles.

Far from the industry norm, she invited fans into each of her homes for intimate album release parties and she bought them Christmas/Hanukkah presents, wrapped them herself, and even delivered some personally! Her fans called it "Swiftmas." (Watch the video clip at laurabull.com with your All Access pass.) This video (image) proves just how much she has dedicated her resources to building a strong brand community, and with these types of activities, she is super-serving them to create the ultimate brand loyalty. If this was another artist, it may come across as contrived, but since we can trace this type of behavior back to the days of Myspace, the tactic is branding gold. It's authentic and seems selfless even though she benefits greatly.

After dissecting Taylor's music, image, and personality we are left with the core pillars of her brand matrix, the unique point within the data that forms a clear and competitive brand.

Now, let's see if you can identify another brand using these three major components: product, image, and narrative. Remember, we are not building your brand yet. We are merely trying to learn how to distinguish the elements of any brand already in the marketplace.

EXERCISE

DISSECTING A BRAND

1. On a sheet of paper, write a successful influencer's name. Someone you admire or someone who is an icon. Withstand the temptation to work on your own brand or on the brand of someone who is in direct competition with you. We are simply dissecting a brand here, not creating one.
2. Begin your brainstorming by listing five adjectives that describe that person's product, five adjectives that describe their image, and five adjectives to describe their personality.
I will do this exercise with you with my own influencer.
My example:

- Product: provocative, rap, materialism, confidence, political
- Image: fashion, colorful, futuristic, designer, clean-cut
- Personality: audacious, outspoken, political, self-efficacy, extravagant

3. Just as we did in the Taylor Swift example above, let's narrow down these terms by finding and circling all the similar adjectives that appear across all three lines. First up: provocative, futuristic, audacious, outspoken, political, and extravagant.

4. Circle the next group of words in a new color: rap could go with political, colorful, outspoken. Use your best judgment.

5. Circle the next category in a new color: materialism, fashion, designer, extravagant.

6. Circle the next category in a new color: confidence, self-efficacy, outspoken.

7. Continue until you've found all the similarities and then cross out any terms that are not found on all three lines (i.e.: clean-cut). Now find ONE TERM that will encompass each colored grouping in the best and most accurate way.

I have Audacious, Outspoken, Provocative, Fashionable

Can you guess who it is? Looking over your own terms, do they accurately reflect your subject? Make sure they would be in the center of our Venn diagram by pulling from all three lines.

At this stage, narrowing the terms down to five under each brand component can be challenging. You need to become a ruthless editor finding the lowest common denominators. Determine which ones have real substance by covering up the influencer's name and asking yourself if anyone would be able to determine who you were describing merely by the terms you've chosen. You are looking for a unique matrix that only defines that specific influencer, and no one else. For instance, if you wrote down "powerhouse vocalist," that term could describe many artists: Martina McBride, Carrie Underwood, Whitney Houston, Adele, just to name a few. However, if you included other key terms like *mod* and/or *British*, the possibilities dwindle until we are left with Adele. Now, review the matrix of terms I chose. Who is my influencer?

That's right. How could we have already been done with Kanye?

His brand is that of a fashionably provocative rapper who is audaciously outspoken about social and political norms. This is a brand that not only survived but thrived after a faux pas like his outburst at the *VMAs* and comments like "George Bush hates black people." Kanye is far from traditional, and he is assertive in his opinions, values, and lifestyle. A conventional publicist would be in constant damage-control mode; a good publicist who understands his brand would let Kanye be Kanye.

Note that in our exercise, we replace the term narrative with personality, because in order to maintain brand authenticity we must analyze the artist's morals/beliefs/lifestyle. The narrative tells who the artist is, not what they've done. Be careful to avoid terms like iconic or superstar. They may have become superstars because of a well-defined brand, but being a superstar is not an element of that brand. The Beatles and Johnny Cash are among a very select few at the upper echelon who rebranded to include the term icon many years into their already successful careers. They did not begin their careers as icons. No one with icon as a core element could have begun his or her career in the past decade.

Another aspect to think about when brainstorming elements of a brand is the need to use only positive vocabulary. There's no use in building a brand with negative connotations if you want it to sell. I chose Kanye to prove that although he is polarizing, he still celebrates a massive fan base that finds the potentially adverse elements enlightening. For instance, I use materialism in the sense of societal and economic commentary in his lyrics, not in the negative sense that would imply he is shallow. I also use audacious instead of reckless or arrogant, which lends a bold and daring tone instead of a thoughtless and conceited one. Our job is to accentuate the positives to our target audience, so spin those negatives around.

Lastly, you want to avoid using media outlets as a descriptive element. You may think of the Super Bowl when you think of Whitney Houston or Saturday Night Live when you think of Justin Timberlake, but these are merely conduits to communicate the brand to the audience and therefore cannot be the brand itself. Saturday Night Live is a point in the communication channel between the brand and its audience, but not the message being delivered. Instead, write down what you witnessed during that show or performance: Was it a sequined jacket, sarcastic humor, or dancing sharks that stood out?

But wait! Does this work for everyone?

YES!

Why?

The possibilities for creating an authentic brand matrix are infinite.

It may take time to find the perfect match, but it does exist for everyone. If you think a brand is sounding too much like a competitor, all you have to do is come up with the one or two unique elements that set you apart. That small shift in the matrix is all it takes to create a unique brand.

Remember our discussion about Oprah? She was the first

African-American female self-made billionaire. Self-awareness, self-forgiveness, and self-efficacy are her cornerstones. Oprah stands for self-enlightenment and spirituality. From the topics on her show to the books suggested for her book club to becoming the spokesperson of Weight Watchers, now called WW International, these themes prevail. Therefore, her brand should look something like this:

Oprah is an African-American lifestyle personality who promotes self-enlightenment, self-esteem, and self-efficacy through inclusion, empowerment, and spirituality.

Notice what's missing and why:

1. She is an icon/mogul/pioneer. True, but she wasn't when she started out. Do not confuse cause and effect.
2. She utilizes television, book clubs, magazines, and more. True, but these are the outlets she uses to deliver her brand, not elements of her brand.
3. She's influential. Again, she is influential because of a strong, authentic, and relatable brand. It's cause versus effect.
4. She's a billionaire. Who cares? Again, cause versus effect.
5. Personal bias. My personal opinions about the brand are not relevant and should be removed from the equation altogether. The goal is to back up the observations with data.
6. Wait. Why does her race need to be included here and not for Taylor or Kanye? For Oprah, this is a defining characteristic. You'll read more about that later.

Ask why each word in the above statement is central to who she is and what she stands for. How does each word facilitate a unique matrix that sets her apart from other lifestyle brands? How has she been able to grow and evolve her business using the same core values/traits over an almost forty-year span?

Looking at Oprah, Taylor, and Kanye, do you believe that any of these brands were created in a boardroom? I'm asked fairly often about which comes first: Does the life dictate the brand or does the brand dictate the life? Does a committee determine how someone should be or act based on the target audience? While I have witnessed narratives made up in a boardroom work for a short period of time, they never last more than a few years at most because of authenticity issues.

Conversely, core elements that are authentic are easy to maintain in public. Although there must be a reciprocal relationship between the two, **it is vital that the identity comes before the brand.** The brand narrative is derived from elements that already exist in the subject's lifestyle/personality.

Taylor Swift, like Oprah, is a savvy businesswoman who understands that she is her brand. She lives her life according to her core pillars. The audience doesn't witness Taylor going to clubs with other starlets; she prefers private homier settings when she's entertaining. The audience doesn't witness Taylor doing drugs or peeing into mop buckets (I'm looking at you, Justin Bieber). The audience doesn't see her getting tattoos, or shaving her head, or wearing barely-there attire, because she knows that her lifestyle is intrinsically linked to her brand.

WHAT'S NEXT?

You now have the ability to recognize successful influencer brands. You can discern how elements of a brand work together to create the brand matrix. However, do not become obsessed with the idea of pinpointing your own core elements yet, as the next few chapters will help to explain how to sift through the vast human complexities that make you unique. Instead, focus on the basics:

- Run through the exercise in this chapter using at least three to five influencers in the same industry as yourself. If you are a blogger, look at successful bloggers; if you are a politician, start picking apart successful leaders. Do not look at any brands created in the past five years; instead, focus on brands that are proven, long-term winners.

- See if you can create a brand statement for the brands you choose. Study the important components and make sure someone you share the statement with could understand that brand and everything it stands for with just one to two sentences. Begin with "So and so is a _____" and don't forget to include what the product is (music, politics, art, fashion, photography, whatever). Let's recap:

  o Taylor Swift is a charming storyteller, an affable and earnest girl next door who shares stories about her life and personal relationships through her music.

  o Kanye West is a fashionably provocative rapper who is audaciously outspoken about social and political norms.

  o Oprah is an African-American lifestyle personality who promotes self-enlightenment, self-esteem, and self-efficacy through inclusion, empowerment, and spirituality.

— 6 —

BEYOND THE IT FACTOR

●●●●

The bus creaked to a lazy halt in front of the Sony Music Entertainment building on Music Row. This wasn't the typical bus that sat in front of a record label waiting for its owner inside, but a charter bus made for church outings and transporting high school footballers to state playoffs. Twelve music hopefuls remained hidden on board as the TV crew feverishly prepped for their arrival inside the building.

The Sony marketing team milled around in the ransacked conference room. Our haven, where we spent most of our days, was unrecognizable. The large table that just hours earlier sat in the shape of a U had lost its midsection and two rows of seats were now flanking each side. The corners of the room housed large stage lamps to set the room on fire, but strategically placed to remain invisible on screen. The room buzzed with the noise of techs testing lapel mics and clipping them on the anxious executives who were going to be on television for the first time.

"Where do you want us?"

"Assemble yourselves like you would for a meeting," suggested the director as he hurried past. "Once everyone from Sony is seated, we'll bring in the contestants and seat them across from you. We'll be filming, so just look natural as they walk in. Give them a speech about what it's like to be a recording artist here and what a big deal that is. Make sure you name some of your bigger artists. If you mess up, we can do another take. Just act normal."

Just act normal. So this is reality TV, I thought. I took the seat behind my boss hoping I'd be able to hide from the camera, as I wasn't quite sure what kind of normal they were looking for.

Thirty minutes later, the director yelled, "Action!"

Twelve hopefuls walked into the room and took their seats facing us. It looked and felt like a duel.

I tuned out as my boss gave his prepared spiel. Instead my attention went to the nervous group of artists with blank stares. This was their big shot, the legendary break everyone dreams of.

Each contestant had a unique look. Their ages spanned decades. You could tell some had been working toward this moment for a long time. I'm sure they could all sing, since they had made it this far in the competition, but who would stand out in this crowd? Who would win the coveted prize, a Nashville recording contract?

This was 2003, and I had only been with the company a few years as the lowly marketing coordinator.

I still believed in the nebulous *it* factor. Actually, most of my coworkers did, too. That's what we were looking for across the room that day. We never found it, and that wasn't our job. Because, in a room of outliers, how do you place that kind of bet? You don't. Instead, you let America decide.

The artist who won the record deal that inaugural season of USA Network's *Nashville Star* was Buddy Jewell, a salt-of-the-earth, forty-one-year-old traditional country singer. His voice was like butter and we released a song that is one of my favorites to this day, "Sweet Southern Comfort." However, even though he won the competition, the novelty wore off a few singles in, and Sony dropped Buddy from the artist roster due to lack of radio airplay. There was some confusion over what Buddy's music should sound like, thematically and sonically. He had been around town for ages trying to secure a record deal, so he went along with everyone's suggestions. That ultimately caused a weak brand to become muddled, and Buddy faded back into obscurity.

There was another artist sitting in that roomful of hopefuls on that first day of filming. She was just eighteen years old, with a Texas-sized chip on her shoulder and enough self-confidence to stand for something. She had never experienced failure on a professional level, and she was just naive enough to tell us record label folk where to stick it. In the beginning stages of her yet-undefined brand, no one in the room, not even she, could have known that in just a few short years she would be the most celebrated female artist in the history of country music. That artist was Miranda Lambert.

●●●●

A mong all the artists I have encountered in my twenty-plus years in the music industry, no one has had a clearer vision of herself and her brand than Miranda Lambert. Like her iconic logo, she is a loaded pistol and a free spirit. She's laid-back, a homebody who loves to be in jeans on a dirt road, but then turns pink and glittery on a red carpet. She's a big advocate for mistreated and abandoned animals, even though she's an avid hunter. She would happily tell someone off for insulting anyone she loves or anything she stands for, and in the next breath, she'll reveal her true vulnerable self as she oozes with empathy.

Miranda has always had a distinct perception of the world, and that insight is prevalent in her music, which is the product that she offers to her consumers. As a young woman, she successfully convinced the head of a major record label to let her take control over her own music before he even signed her. That's unheard of, and it's a testament to how powerful someone can be when they identify deeply with their brand. The beautiful thing is that her boldness has only strengthened over time, as she has built up unshakable self-confidence.

Having a clear sense of the product and the appropriate form that product should take is the first step in developing a viable company. A product is a tangible commodity or service provided to the customer: It can be a speech, music, art, a photograph, a blog, a live show, a stand-up routine, a novel, fashion, food, merchandise, a television series, and the list goes on and on. Hang on, you say, how is a speech a product?

When politicians orate, they are selling their policies and promises, and the public buys these with a vote. A money exchange is not necessary, as a vote is more valuable to a politician. Similarly, a content creator (a politically correct term for online blogger) needs their followers to click and Like and share. Neither consumer is spending money, but it allows the influencer to gain power, which will lead to income from sponsorships, secondary products, and even fund-raising.

Yes, the politician must sell herself first for a proper buy-in from her followers. That is the entire premise of this book. However, the policies are the actionable and quantifiable product and a speech is the form chosen to present those policies to the consumers. Other forms that would do well selling a politician's *policies* may be a book or a blog. Remember the perfume bottle? The perfume is the form of the product; the unique scent, the chemical composition, is the product. Therefore, we can sell that scent in many different forms. Will that scent sell better as a perfume or as a lotion, or maybe even a candle? Your brand statement will tell you the answer.

Miranda Lambert began by selling her product, which, of course, is her music, in the form of albums and live shows, the standard for all musicians. An album is a tangible commodity and the live show is a service that provides an experience. Both exist to sell the music, a chemical composition created from her themes, tones, mood, and, in Miranda's case, an East Texas drawl. Once these unique elements are put together, Miranda's sound is like nothing else on the radio. It could have come only from her.

If you've picked up this book, you have some sense of what your core product may be. Are you a producer creating techno beats? Are you a blogger pushing environmental strategies, or a photographer selling black-and-white prints? If you're a photographer, what are you shooting? Landscapes? Portraits? Do you have unique themes or lighting techniques? Whatever commodity you have decided to present, at this point you realize that first and foremost, as an influencer, **the product must be a derivative of your purpose**. That purpose is yours alone.

Secondly, that product or service must be superior to others on the market.

Your peers are not the competition; the competition is the person who is already a superstar.

Ask yourself, what do you do better than Miranda Lambert? What do you do better than Oprah? Pull out those notes with your passions and strengths and focus on those attributes. You have a unique point of view from a lifetime of experiences, which no one else can replicate.

Life coach Marie Forleo preaches, "No other person ever has, or ever will have, the unique blend of talents, strengths, and perspective that you have." Even if doubt arises, because it doesn't look like there is room in the marketplace for your product, know that's not true. Forleo encounters these doubts frequently with her entrepreneurial clients. In rebuttal she points to Beyoncé.

Imagine if Mrs. Knowles-Carter had chosen not to release music from Destiny's Child because the marketplace was already crowded with female bands. Back in the 1990s, music fans adored R&B girl band TLC, and the Spice Girls claimed world domination. However, these three brands could not be farther from each other on the musical spectrum, and the marketplace had room for each. Destiny's Child had a unique product shared in a unique way to a unique segment of the market, which earned the group millions before they disbanded and Beyoncé catapulted into superstardom.

One way to fine-tune your product is to categorize your tangible good or service within the marketplace. We can place Miranda in many marketable categories; the further you dig, the better off your product will be. For instance, Miranda's product falls under the vast umbrella of the entertainment industry; within that arena, she resides in the music category. Digging further still, she's a country music singer. How about a female country singer from Texas? How about a female country singer-songwriter from East Texas with influences of Merle Haggard and John Prine? Are we narrowing down her product? Are we eliminating possible competition? You could go on, and you should. Be bold and create an entirely new category!

Wherever you land will determine a lot about how you market your product. You will know which retailers to target, the audience to woo, and even what you should charge. And, in a little bit of a "what comes first: the chicken or the egg" scenario, that category will also dictate the form your product should take.

BE A SHARK!

My husband and I are avid *Shark Tank* marathoners, the reality show where novice entrepreneurs pitch their companies to a panel of millionaire (and billionaire) investors. I'm pretty sure we've seen every episode with tech geeks Mark Cuban and Robert Herjavec, licensing tough-guy Mr. Wonderful, retail and marketing guru Lori Greiner, fashion mogul Daymond John, and mega-Realtor Barbara Corcoran. The show offers great lessons to entrepreneurs on how to pitch a company for seed money, and often the focus of the pitch becomes about the viability of the products themselves. Does the consumer need the product? Usually, for influencers, that answer is no. We aren't selling eggs and flour; we are selling art, music, and items that could make someone happier with their lives. These are not necessities, but there's hope.

**Influencers don't necessarily have to fill a need,
but they need to fill a want.**

Many of the amazing products pitched on *Shark Tank* are nowhere near necessities, yet my husband and I have purchased many of them. For instance, I've purchased the Scrub Daddy, which has been touted as the show's biggest success with more than $50 million in sales. Regular sponges are just fine, but how cool is a bright yellow, smiling sponge that changes firmness with water temperature? Or my favorite, the $40 Zipadee-Zip: a swaddle for infants. My baby girl is currently snoring while wrapped in the ultra-delicate, wearable blanket created by a stay-at-home mom from her kitchen table. There are twenty other swaddles on the market, none of which are necessities. But I want thirty extra minutes of writing time, so I'm going to use the swaddle that makes my baby girl sleep the longest. After trying three other brands, Shark Tank helped us discover the winner.

Frequent *Shark Tank* guest and Skinnygirl Global founder Bethenny Frankel said on a recent episode that she simply created a cocktail, which by no means is a novel concept or a necessity. There are thousands of other bottled cocktails flooding liquor store shelves; it's an incredibly difficult store shelf to conquer. But, with Skinnygirl, Bethenny created an entirely new subset of an industry that has focused entirely too long on male shoppers.

How did such a simple product revolutionize an industry? The Skinnygirl Margarita has one-fifth of the calories of its competitors. Women everywhere rejoiced. No one needs a Skinnygirl Margarita, but they sure want one at the end of a crappy day. And, if they are already cheating on a diet with alcohol, they might as well make sure their thighs still squeeze into blue jeans the next morning.

Giving the audience what they want can be more powerful than giving them what they need.

Having said that, influencers must ask themselves whether their product is a hobby or a viable business venture. On *Shark Tank*, the investors poke and prod, ask about sales and liabilities, uncover backstories and passions, and ultimately decide whether or not to invest. Nine times out of ten, the ones who leave with an unchanged bank account are the ones who have a hobby on their hands.

A hobby needs passion; a business needs passion and consumers.

With society's growing acceptance of side hustles, the difference is important to note. Will people want your product? Why? An idea may be something the business owner wants, but the marketplace must follow.

The only way to know if the product is a need, a want, or a hobby is to remain objective. When I was at Sony, the most-asked question around the boardroom table was, "What should the next single be?" The decision on which song should be shipped to radio could earn or lose the company millions of dollars and potentially make or break careers. It is a major investment decision and one that cannot be answered with subjective opinions. In a room with ten executives discussing an album with ten songs, there could be ten different favorites.

Instead, I learned to remove my personal feelings from the equation and ask what our consumer would want. At the time our core audience shopped—no, lived—at Walmart. They were forty-year-old soccer moms who valued God, America, and their families. They were blue collar and Southern (not necessarily geographically). If we released a song with a Christian theme, it became a hit. Think

Carrie Underwood's "Jesus, Take the Wheel," Brooks & Dunn's "Believe," and Brad Paisley's "When I Get Where I'm Going," to name a few. If we released a song with an American theme, it became a hit. Remember Underwood's "All-American Girl," Brooks & Dunn's "Only in America," and Paisley's "American Saturday Night"?

There were many times that I could not identify with our customer base. In fact, if it had been up to me, Sony never would have signed Kenny Chesney. Gasp! Nothing against him at all. He's a great guy and a brilliant marketer. I just prefer my country a little more roots and a little less beachy. Yet, as I busied myself organizing an industry-wide party to commemorate Chesney's sale of 25 million albums, complete with Kenny's favorite reggae band, I realized I probably shouldn't make business decisions on what I would buy.

Even if an influencer is spot-on the same demographic as those they are targeting, which is most likely the case if they are effectively using the principles of influence, they are still not the consumer. With background knowledge, we know too much about how the sausage was made, so to speak. That, in addition to heavy emotional baggage, will cloud judgment. A smart influencer has studied the industry, sized up the competition, and learned the best manipulation tactics for their product. That insider information can become blinding during the marketing process, so it is always best to remain objective.

DISCOVERING THE CORE AUDIENCE

Most consumers are passive shoppers. They are too busy with the rush of the daily grind and too overwhelmed by the explosion of the Information Age. Marketers have to constantly hit consumers with the same messages over and over again before they absorb the information and act on it. Think of a hit song you are currently obsessed with. Do you remember the first time you heard it? Probably not, because the first few times we hear something, we don't actually listen.

At first, consumers are attracted only by surface attributes like catchy lyrics or a high-energy beat. Once the subliminal decision is made that we like those surface elements, the song moves into our consciousness. After many impressions, we begin to process deeper elements, like meaning.

Focus groups believed that Sugarland's "Stay" was about a woman asking her cheating husband to come home. In reality the song was about a mistress wanting her married boyfriend to leave his wife, a risky theme in a consumer pool dedicated to Christian lifestyles. Yet it sold millions. The consumers never listened carefully enough to the lyrics to understand what the song was about. They were drawn in by the mood the melody created. This is surface level.

As the story goes, Sara Bareilles's label refused to release her album, feeling it was missing a hit love song. Despondent and exasperated, she retreated to the studio and penned "Love Song." Her lyrics about "staring at blank pages" with her "head under water" is a cry for creative freedom and a "f--- you" to her record label. The single became the fifth most played song of 2008, launching her career and making millions. To this day, the majority of the audience couldn't tell you what that song is really about.

This reaction could be surface or it could be that the lyrics were taken as metaphor. Either way, the false perceptions of these tunes proves that unless a brand comes out of the gate with amazing clarity and an intense emotional connection, the consumers may not react consciously without experiencing repeated impressions. To combat consumer indifference and to save time and money, marketers must decide which segments of the population will be their core audience.

Pinpointing an audience is an art form.

Creatives tend to shy away from anything that sounds like analytical data, but deciphering who the audience is, how to reach them, and what message would best resonate is a creative endeavor. The more that is discovered about the core base, the more creative the marketing strategy can become. The possibilities are endless.

I'm sure, by now, you've heard we Texans are pickup truck–driving, horse-riding, farm-living country folk. This accurately describes a large segment of the Texas population. We call all sodas Coke, we float the Guadalupe, and we're fully aware of our right to secede from the union if those DC politicians go off the rails. You will see the Texas flag down here more than the American flag, although both get the utmost respect.

These are Miranda's people. This is how Miranda grew up, in a small East Texas town. Now, before I get hate mail, understand that Texas is large. It takes thirteen hours to drive across the state without traffic or rest stops from both north to south *and* east to west. Our major cities are stocked full of young millennial white-collar workers and skyscrapers. I drive an SUV and live in a Dallas suburb, but I know Miranda's people—my family members among them—so I know how and why they buy.

They shop at Walmart, they listen to small-town radio stations, they prefer dive bars and line dancing over nightclubs, and they buy Miranda Lambert music. This consumer data tells us where to sell and how to promote in order to achieve the best results. How about a partnership with Dr Pepper, Tractor Supply Company, or even the Texas Parks & Wildlife Department? Did you know that almost every pickup truck manufacturer in the US has a Texas edition? All of these brands would put Miranda front and center with a demographic that yields a high probability of acting on a purchase. Bottom line: A company can spend millions of wasted dollars trying to successfully reach the mass market (everyone) hoping to capture consumers who may be interested, or they can narrow their target market (ideal potential consumers) and sell to them.

To accomplish this, marketers use target market analysis to help establish who their potential customers may be. They ascertain what makes the consumers tick, their wants and needs, culture and lifestyle choices, psychological makeup, and ultimately how they will receive a product. This knowledge will equip a company with valuable information like revenue goals, pricing options, manufacturing projections, and, of course, marketing strategy.

EXERCISE

CHARACTER DEVELOPMENT

In my free time, I like to write fiction. I find that developing characters for a novel is a lot like developing the basis for a target market, as characters tend to be a metaphor for specific populations.

Imagine you are a novelist with a wonderful plot idea. Before you can write the all-important opening line, you must know your characters and their motivations. Who is the protagonist? How would this person react in this difficult circumstance? Why? Strong character development enables a realistic plotline, which moves the story along.

Think about the life of Harry Potter and why an eleven-year-old orphan takes on the all-powerful Voldemort. Think about Jay Gatsby, or Elizabeth Bennet, or Jo March. Who are

continued

these characters? What are their hopes and dreams, their pasts, their failures and successes, their battles both internal and external? Where are they from, and how do they interact with the world? Can these character specifics predict their future?

Grab about five blank pages and ask yourself questions about your protagonist. The only thing you know about the person is that they are a core consumer of your product. Now let's flesh them out. What's their age, gender, vocation, and location? Who are their parents and grandparents, and what did they do for a living? Are they rich or poor, religious or atheist, educated and/or cultured? Who are their best friends and why? What are their hobbies and lifestyle choices? What's their favorite store and how do they prefer to make purchases? What does a day in the life entail? Who *are* they?

Write for as long as you can, using the free-association technique. This is brainstorming, and you can focus on specifics or edits later. Take the time to understand who this person is and what makes them tick. Once you have completed a thorough character development, these are the most important questions to ask:

1. Does this person need and/or want my product?
2. Why?

If the answer is yes to number one and you know why, you may have just found your target market.

Today, with online marketing, influencers are able to target markets in unprecedented ways. Television and radio are great for mass marketing, but if there's a limited budget, social media is the ticket. The level of specification is astounding. A marketer can run a direct response campaign to hit thirty-to-forty-year-old males in the 75023 zip code who like trucks and listen to country music.

Knowing the target market will also fuel decisions regarding where to sell products and how. Did you know that grocery stores put sugary cereals closer to the floor? They don't do that to make sure you get a good workout. This is a ploy to attract little kids who will pick them up and ask mommy to buy them. They are being marketed directly to children.

Taking a drive down any local highway, it is hard not to notice all of the large fast food signs like Burger King, Popeyes, In-N-Out Burger, Wendy's, and McDonald's. Have you ever noticed the one similarity common to all of them? They are all different shapes and sizes, but the majority of all fast food logos incorporate the color red. Yes, this vibrant color stands out well against the blue sky, but beyond that, research shows that red stimulates hunger, proving again that if you know your consumer, you will know where and how you should market your product in order to elicit a positive response.

The most important reason to find a target audience, however, may be to help protect your ego. You will never be able to please everyone, and if you try, you will end up losing yourself completely. There will be plenty of people in the world who dislike everything about your brand, and since your brand so closely resembles the very core of who you are as a person, that will sting. Some influencers have decided to avoid direct consumer feedback on social media altogether, which may result in the loss of valuable information.

By doing a target market analysis, you identify those who will most likely love what you have to offer.

Confidence in the product and confidence in the audience results in confidence in yourself.

So, once you know whose opinion truly matters, it is safe to move on to image and narrative.

FAIL FAST

Looking at market data and listening to what the target demographic wants will always dictate what an influencer offers to their followers. Consumers will reveal whether a product is viable. The trick is to listen and listen often. If they are buying and sharing and Liking, that product has hit the mark and the influencer should increase marketing efforts for that product. If the audience and revenue keep growing, the product or service is a winner.

If, on the other hand, the consumers are rejecting the commodity, it's wise to get into a Fail Fast mode. Even if they aren't interacting, **please understand that no response is a response**. An element of the overall brand is not making sense to the consumer. It could be the product, the image, or the narrative. By failing fast, an influencer will save valuable resources and bounce back quickly with something that does work. Doing so ensures that the majority of consumers won't even know there was a misstep.

WHAT'S NEXT?

It is imperative to know right now, at this moment, before going any further, what you are going to sell and how to reach your target audience. Knowing your audience may not necessarily alter your product, but it may alter how you present that product through image and narrative. And for guidance on those topics, keep reading.

- Determine what you are selling. What is the core product and what is the best form to begin with out of the gate? What is the chemical composition that makes your core product unique? How is your purpose reflected in that product? Dig deep and be authentic.
- How would you classify your core product?
- List ten direct competitors. Remember, these are the current superstars, not your peers.
- Ask yourself, does this product fill a need or a want?
- Determine who your target audience is by doing the target analysis worksheet on my website, laurabull.com.
- Have a Fail Fast backup plan that you can implement quickly.

—7—

A LASTING IMPRESSION

• • • •

*"I take the South with me everywhere I go, . . . It's
become sort of an obsession of mine, spreading the gospel
of southern living. My southern heritage informs my
whole life—how I value generosity, how I decorate my
house, and how I make holidays special for my kids—not
to mention how I talk, dance, and do my hair . . ."*

—Reese Witherspoon, actress, producer,
founder of lifestyle brand Draper James,
and author of *Whiskey in a Teacup*

• • • •

Few people understand the power of a visual more than actors. They gain weight, dye hair, and don prosthetics to reveal the essence of a character. In addition to dialogue, they rely on everything from physicality to wardrobe and lighting to make their stories authentic on film. In *Legally Blonde*, Elle Woods flits around Harvard in a bubble of bright pink with an overly optimistic and sometimes naive manner. She's a fish out of water but is comfortable in her stilettos. In *Wild*, Cheryl Strayed limps along mountain trails in ratty clothes, with ratty hair, and ratty luck. She is practically suffocated by the weight of the pack she carries, a metaphor for the pressures of the world and her longing to escape. In *Sweet Home Alabama*, Melanie Carmichael's last name isn't the only thing that changes as the character evolves. Her wardrobe transforms from classy and bold to casual and soft as her accent evolves from nondescript to a thick Southern drawl.

The visual representation of these characters is necessary for the audience to understand the story. Why? The philosophical explanation is that the world around us is only the world as we perceive it. The colors and smells and tastes are unique to our past experiences. And as one of the most powerful senses, vision allows our brains to scan the world and register a reaction based on the elements it understands. If Cheryl Strayed had hiked 1,100 miles of the Pacific Crest Trail in designer clothes and perfectly coiffed hair, we would cry foul. That visual does not ring true to our own experiences of camping and nature. The experience is tied to the visual and vice versa.

After a career playing these and other characters, Oscar-winning actress Reese Witherspoon has recently embarked on her most authentic role yet as the founder of the lifestyle brand Draper James. The brand's product lines project the lifestyle that Reese has lived and valued since childhood. How does her clothing line visually represent all that lovely grace and charm? Through lace details, conservative cuts, and floral prints, of course. How does a store suggest an upscale Southern lifestyle? By offering the perfect outfits for ladies who lunch, pink trinket trays adorned with the motto Strong, Sweet, and Southern, and tote bags stamped with "Hello, Sugar" or "What would Dolly do?" all at boutique pricing (think $100 and up). The products are the clothing and accessories, the image tells us a story, and the brand sells us a lifestyle.

Now, even though Reese graces the screen in the guise of other characters, her real offscreen persona is where we find her brand. She was born in New Orleans, grew up in Nashville, and attended Harpeth Hall, an all-girl private preparatory school. She was the daughter of two PhDs and granddaughter of socialites. Her Southern roots reveal themselves every time she appears on television through her warm, charming, and respectful banter. She even wrote the best-selling *Whiskey in a Teacup* to teach us all the ins and outs of proper Southern living, from how to master hot rollers to throwing the best mint julep–soaked Kentucky Derby parties.

Reese Witherspoon wears Draper James's styles because she is a Southern lady. Her clothing is a visual representation of her lifestyle, her beliefs and values, and her personality. She sells it because she's proud of those values and knows other Southern ladies will appreciate them too. When you grow up in small-town America where everyone knows everyone and beauty shop gossip is the last word, it becomes apparent how essential appearances can be.

FIRST IMPRESSIONS ARE IMPORTANT; LASTING IMPRESSIONS ARE EVERYTHING

A team of neuroscientists at MIT found that the human brain processes images in just a few milliseconds. The amygdala, the section of the brain that handles social interactions, decides if someone is trustworthy before the rest of the brain can even process the face. This means that before you even introduce yourself, I have made judgments based on your looks alone. This also means that when you open a magazine to a Gucci ad, you have judged the model, the clothing, and the designer in less than one second.

I often run focus groups for influencers to find out more about how the consumer perceives the brand. In those sessions, I display a primary image and solicit feedback on how the audience thinks and feels about that image without any background knowledge like what the influencer does or even their name. I ask about tone and mood and how the image makes them feel. I ask the group to tell me a story based on the image alone: who are they with, what are they doing, who is this person? They respond with what type of car they imagine the influencer drives, what drink they prefer, and what type of activities they do in their spare time, all by viewing one image, often a tight close-up.

This exercise allows me to test the brand's identity in the absence of a voice. I once put up a female musician's image. She was lounging in a rusted red outdoor chair, barefoot, wearing skinny jeans and a loose-fitting striped flannel shirt, with her arm draped casually over the chair. She was laughing, and her gaze was off camera, but her body faced the audience. She looked like she was in mid-conversation, hanging out on someone's backyard patio. There was not one instrument in the photo, or anything identifying her as a musician.

Pretty quickly, the focus group got in a debate about whether she drank white wine or Bud Light. The happiness she conveyed through the image and her relaxed style suggested to the women in the room that she was one of them; she was with her gal pals sipping on white wine and sharing gossip. The guys in the group saw the same image and felt she was one of them, hanging out on a friend's patio drinking a beer and shootin' the shit. There wasn't any drink in her hand, no subliminal alcohol signs in the image, yet the debate got rather heated, with both sides intent on taking ownership over the brand identity. Each side had developed a narrative based on what made sense in the context of their own perception of the world.

The good news for us was that they were both right. This client enjoyed Bud Light at dive bars just as much as classing it up with a glass of white wine for a girl's night out. She appealed to both men and women of all ages in the focus group without playing one note of her music and without revealing one thing about her personality. No one in the room that day said she sipped aged Irish whiskey or threw back chilled Mexican tequila, which means we were doing something right. The closer the test group is to picking up on the story the image is aiming to express, the closer we are to success.

Sometimes, when we present an image during these sessions, a few decide they dislike the influencer within seconds. Their amygdalas make a snap decision based on the viewers' preconceptions. Within the first few questions, it becomes apparent that they have made a negative judgment but cannot express why until they take the time to think it over and talk it out. Answers like "I don't know, I just don't like it" or "That's not someone I would be friends with" lead to the question, why?

Digging deeper allows us to find the psychological reasoning behind that reaction. The first impression taints their opinion and it becomes a struggle to free them from the negative tone and return their brain to neutral. Remember, the happiness advantage says the brain is more creative and more open-minded in a neutral or positive state, therefore the brain at negative is closed off. A negative first impression is hard to remedy.

A group that begins at neutral or positive, on the other hand, tends to be the most accurate regarding the influencer's true brand. They are quicker at assessing the image and more open to the possible connections they may have with the person depicted. This proves that a good first impression allows the audience to be open to the possibility of a positive lasting impression, which translates into long-term brand loyalty.

The overall goal in developing a great image is to achieve that long-term brand loyalty. This requires either an over-the-top or a neutral/positive first impression followed by many subsequent positive impressions. Imagine a man drops to one knee and opens his hand to reveal a small, robin's egg blue box. Yippee! It's a diamond ring from Tiffany & Co.! That robin's egg blue box is so synonymous with their luxury jewelry that the company trademarked the color. One simple element of image, the color, partnered with one amazing moment, has translated to a lasting positive feeling about the brand.

Likewise, being exposed to repetitive positive impressions is conducive to long-term brand loyalty. My best childhood friend, Jessica, the one with the Paula Abdul shirt, received many gifts from Tiffany's for birthdays, holidays, and other celebrations. Her parents are addicted to giving gifts bought at Tiffany's, which I can completely get behind, and each left a positive impression on their daughter, resulting in a lifelong affinity to the brand.

THE INFLUENCER'S IMAGE

Audrey Hepburn was a master of creating an image. Today, seven decades after the height of her career, her creation is still ingrained in our psyche. Her name is synonymous with her effervescent, French-inspired, tomboyesque, 1960s mod style: pixie hair, slim black pants, and ballet flats, which turned fashion into a feminist statement.

The Belgian-born actress was known for her European flair and classy style. She was drawn to roles that allowed her to showcase these elements of her image, such as a European princess in *Roman Holiday*, the sophisticated socialite/escort in *Breakfast at Tiffany's*, and the title character in 1954's *Sabrina*.

Audrey pioneered the art of turning fashion into a personal statement. She believed that everyone should have a unique image, as everyone has a unique story to tell. This is true for all influencers. The image combines visual elements to portray the product in such a way that it effectively tells its story to the consumer. There are endless possibilities of visual elements to choose from, like package design, logos, colors, fonts, wardrobe, filters, makeup, haircut and color, lighting, even the car someone drives. Here are some examples of visual brand stories:

- Bruno Mars's band wearing matching suits
- Pink's pink hair
- Katy Perry's left shark
- Lady Gaga's meat dress
- Sia's face-covering wig
- Johnny Cash's black suit
- Kim Kardashian's curve-hugging wardrobe

All of these visual elements tell the audience something about the influencer's brand through mediums like video, photos, performances, books, artwork, posters, websites, and more. Bruno's band's suits showcase the retro elements of his music; Pink's hair shows she's a rebel; Katy's shark helps create her hyper circus atmosphere; Gaga likes to shock, so why not wear meat; Sia would rather you appreciate the music, not her looks; Cash is a badass and can wear whatever he wants; and Kardashian oozes body confidence. When these elements are paired with other accented features within the matrix, a unique story begins to unfold.

Reese Witherspoon's *Whiskey in a Teacup* features many visual components that work together to tell her life story. The book is an homage to her Nashville socialite grandmother and her love affair with all that's beautiful and authentic about the refined South. The images go beyond her Draper James wardrobe in order to coincide with the book's content. (You should be thinking product = book, narrative = content.) The styled photos, colors, page layouts, and font choices all share Reese's distinct vision of the South of her childhood.

Page after page the reader encounters photos of impeccably maintained gardens, a large equestrian barn, perfectly manicured lawns and grand colonial porches, vintage wallpapers, quilts, and solid brass doorknobs. There are images of her family laughing in the kitchen and on the front porch, Southern hospitality by way of decorating and hosting, and casual sunny afternoons in the garden. Throughout, Reese accessorizes her bright and cheery wardrobe with everything from cowboy boots to Kentucky Derby hats to red lipstick and big hair. The colors are bright and vibrant, like bold pinks, cheerful yellows, all shades of greens and blues. Almost every image includes a vintage touch in the patterns or accessories, the warm hardwoods, and the floral accents.

Without reading one single word of text, these visual elements combined portray an upscale, mid-century Southern lifestyle. Without knowing the author, the reader learns she is warm and inviting and enjoys hosting both casual and formal events for friends and family. She appreciates nature and surrounds herself with activities like gardening, horseback riding, hiking, and playing games in the yard. She has an old soul and old-fashioned charm; she values manners and heritage. The themes of beauty and strength run together just as the title suggests.

This is no happy accident. It takes a highly trained team to pull the multitude of elements together in a cohesive way that ensures the right visual story is presented. Creative directors, stylists, prop and set decorators, photographers and lighting assistants, glam squads, and more work together to find the best way to tell the story.

At the risk of repeating myself to the point of annoying, every single visual element matters to the overall brand. If you don't believe that something as minuscule as a haircut matters to brand identity, just ask actress Keri Russell. Chopping off her long locks during the second season of *Felicity* proved to be a major sticking point with the audience and is now considered one of the worst TV bungles of all time. In fact, it was so bad that networks now include stricter image clauses in contracts, dissuading their stars from making any changes to physical appearance.

I was once in the middle of a heated months-long debate on whether a male artist should cut his hair in order to get more traction on the radio. Another time, it was whether a male artist should ditch the favorite scarf that made him seem more metro than all-American. Yet another time, it was a battle over cowboy hat versus no cowboy hat. It may sound trivial, but these decisions are critical.

It's never just about the hat; it is what the hat says about the brand. It is about whether the hat will help the product stand out in a positive way, whether the consumer will connect with the message as intended. The visual elements and visual mediums must work within the parameters of the core pillars to ensure the brand identity is accurate and effective and able to create long-term brand loyalty.

EXERCISE

CREATIVE DIRECTION

Carrie Bradshaw, star of *Sex and the City*, has been asked to write a book about high-end entertaining in uptown Manhattan

continued

for her audience base of single, professional, thirtysomethings. You have been tasked as creative director and must determine themes and tone as you direct all visual elements. On a separate sheet of paper, break down the following:

What are the themes of the book? Carrie never cooks, so is the focus of the content on club/restaurant openings, showcasing her favorite chefs, or best restaurant patios? What is the tone of Carrie's voice?

Next . . .

List the visual elements that need to be factored in: fonts, colors, hair, makeup, the size of the book, the paper's texture. Everything you can see matters.

Next . . .

Create a mood board by bringing in colors, textures, words that will express your concept visually. What types of restaurants do you have in mind: penthouse views or garden patios in Manhattan? What brings the images together visually? If a major theme is feminism, what are the wardrobe choices that tell the story—soft ruffles or bold satin? What colors will be factored in throughout? Feminine colors like pink, or are you going for a more elegant rose gold? Maybe she's more modern and you choose a bold black-and-white theme.

Review your final mood board. Do the elements tell you a story? If you didn't know any of the book's content or themes, would the visuals alone clue you in?

TRANSFERENCE

One tactic used in advertising quite often is the use of transference, which is the attempt to transfer one's feelings about a product you are familiar with to another product by putting those products together. Many endorsement deals are based on this overall principle: Women think Beyoncé is beautiful, therefore wearing Covergirl will make them beautiful, too. It is a subconscious reaction that occurs when the consumer visually processes the information presented to them.

Audrey Hepburn and Givenchy's partnership is an early example of transference. When Audrey wore the new, up-and-coming designer, her positive brand attributes, like casual femininity, transferred to his brand, and his aristocratic style to hers. By joining together, they created a more powerful narrative for both.

Similarly, Reese's Draper James brand has strategically partnered with Crate & Barrel in a relationship that successfully transfers the positive elements of each brand onto the other. This partnership allows Reese to market her lifestyle brand to the Crate & Barrel audience and allows Crate & Barrel to utilize an influencing powerhouse. Remember, Reese is warm and inviting. She's the hostess with the mostest. She is everyone's best friend. Crate & Barrel is the one-stop shop for those who love to entertain with perfect tablescapes and thoughtful gifts. Their motto is, "To help people love how they live in moments that matter," which, if Reese had a motto, could be hers.

The Crate & Barrel website displays a quote over the Draper James dinnerware collection that simply says, "There's really no wrong way to entertain. XO —Reese." The patterns consist of florals and basketweaves, both in rich monochromatic indigo blue. The images are inspired by Southern style and elegance. The visual elements are similar to the images found in her book, *Whiskey in a Teacup*, and also in the designs of her clothing line.

The Christmas commercial featuring both brands uses the same aesthetic. It showcases three large Christmas trees with lots of wrapped presents and a massive food spread complete with Crate & Barrel products and inviting decor. Reese is wearing a Draper James red polka-dot blouse with a sophisticated pussy bow and bright red lipstick, both illustrating her famous upscale Southern vintage style. She flashes that outsized, enthusiastic smile into the camera and speaks directly to the viewer as if her "soon-to-be bestie" were a guest in her own home.

This campaign, which you can view from my website, is well thought out. In fact it's flawless. The transference is successful because the visual elements make sense to the consumer's perceptions and the positive brand attributes are accented for each brand. The consumers understand the tone, mood, and message. This isn't to say that the retailer partnered with the only influencer that would make sense; another influencer could also work. But, just like the imaginary Home Depot/Beyoncé commercial, if Crate & Barrel had chosen to partner with Oprah, the visual elements would have to be altered to work for both brands.

Nike is another example of a company whose entire Just Do It marketing campaign relies on subconscious transference by pairing world-class athletes with its activewear. The NBA fan associates LeBron James with power and endurance. The audience witnesses LeBron James wearing Nike and they subconsciously transfer those attributes onto the Nike products. Nike's products, therefore, must be powerful and enduring.

Transference is so powerful that it can also transfer negative attributes from one brand to another if one is not careful. Oftentimes, influencers find partnerships dissolved on the other side of scandal to prevent this transfer. Take the now infamous Nike ad with South African Olympian Oscar Pistorius, in which his speed is compared to a bullet in a gun. This ad campaign was live on his website when he was charged with the shooting death of his girlfriend in their South African apartment.

Eerie foreshadowing aside, this obviously sends an awful message about Nike due to no fault of its own. Oscar's brand changed dramatically overnight, and you would expect his negative narrative would have transferred onto Nike, right? But, it didn't. Why?

First, Nike quickly removed the advertisement and dropped Pistorius from their roster. This sends the message to the consumer that they do not condone the behavior of the fallen star athlete. Second, Nike has been successful at diversifying its partnerships. This is a smart tactic when dealing with influencers, because they are more prone to scandal and negative media than a typical company. Nike has forged so many successful partnerships that the failed ones are quickly forgotten. Third, the consumer is not stupid. They understand that the ad campaign made sense when the advertisement was created, and there was no possible way Nike could have foreseen the tragic ending.

When the public watched Pistorius in court as he was found guilty of murder, the consumer was not thinking, man, I really need to throw out my Nike gear. There were no negative residual feelings toward Nike. The negative transference was not permanent, and Nike did not suffer a significant sales drop or long-term damage to the brand. Nike's diverse portfolio of sponsored athletes and the enduring success of the Just Do It campaign protected the company from a brand crisis.

Consumers are not so forgiving, however, when the implied attributes to be transferred are confusing or just plain manufactured. The influencer and partner company will see short-term and potentially long-term damage from this scenario. In the early aughts, for example, Sarah Jessica Parker entered into an advertising campaign with the Gap that proved a sales disaster.

At the time of the collaboration, the public saw Sarah Jessica Parker as synonymous with her iconic role in *Sex and the City*. They thought of her as a New York City fashionista socialite. Styled by Patricia Field, Carrie Bradshaw's wardrobe consisted of outrageous runway designs of barely-there pieces, loud colors, and expensive Christian Louboutin shoes and Louis Vuitton handbags. She wore couture gowns that cost as much as my yearly mortgage payment on her ordinary Friday night out.

Gap's style, however, could not be more polar opposite. Their pieces are plain, staple items that everyday Americans enjoy, certainly not anything you'd find in Carrie Bradshaw's closet. Bradshaw would probably die before donning basic khaki pants, yet here was the actress wearing them with a simple cardigan. The intended transference from Parker to Gap failed miserably, and the partnership left consumers bewildered. The ad campaign fizzled shortly after it began, and both brands experienced a short-term backlash, though both bounced back quickly.

As a notable face of fashion and regular Met Gala attendee, Sarah Jessica Parker soon launched the SJP Collection featuring designer shoes and handbags sold at Bloomingdale's, Saks, and exclusive designer boutiques. The current lookbook of SJP shoe offerings showcases how this venture is more in line with her Carrie Bradshaw image.

ADAPTABLE DESIGN

Just a quick note about adaptable design and how to use it for your benefit. Adaptable design is manipulating the individual visual elements from an overall design campaign and using those same elements, together or separately, on different products, websites, social networks, and more. For instance, *Legally Blonde* uses the same pink font, blue-sky background, and image of Reese in a pink dress walking her chihuahua on all movie posters, trailers, and merchandise. If there is no room for an image, the blue sky with the pink logo appears as the adaptable design, or maybe just the font alone. By repeating these visuals across all assets, the movie marketers are reinforcing the narrative of the movie.

Remember, the average consumer must be exposed to an image/message many times before they act on it. Therefore, by increasing the number of outlets that feature the adaptable design, the greater number of impressions that message will earn, and the greater the chances the consumer will purchase the product.

It's also important that you create a new adaptable design for any product additions. For example, when Taylor Swift's album *Red* was released, all her online assets were branded with the red theme, using visual elements that were incorporated in the album packaging. When she released *1989*, those same assets were rebranded with an 1980s theme that again matched the album package with Polaroid-style graphic design, sepia tones, and a font that looked like Sharpie handwriting. As long as each design rings true to the brand's core pillars, these changes are not only welcome, but necessary to convey the narrative of the new product.

Adaptable design is essential because consumers may favor

different outlets, and we want them to get the same message wherever they search for information. Some prefer Instagram, some may choose Facebook, and others may visit an official website. If different visuals appear on multiple platforms, the opportunity to present one concise message to the consumer is missed. The disconnect in messaging may even confuse those who frequent many different outlets. That one consistent message can inspire a consumer to click rather than scroll past.

WHAT'S NEXT?

- Create a mood board for your brand identity and include as many visual elements as possible (remember the Carrie Bradshaw exercise). See links to some great examples and how-to videos on my website. Take your time and have fun!
- Write down what you believe to be your style. Key words that help define or describe that style should be included in the mood board.
- Share that mood board with a few people to solicit feedback. Go beyond your family and friends and do not reveal any details about the brand. Ask for initial thoughts and feelings based only on the tone, colors, textures, etc. The feedback will clue you in on what may need to be tweaked to better represent your product and narrative.

TIP: Once you are ready to begin capturing your visuals with photography or graphic design, be sure to maintain professionalism by hiring the best team. Stylists, photographers, and many others can bring your mood board to life or they can rob you of a clear and unique image. Do not cut corners with your image. It's your first impression.

TIP: Remember, you are competing with superstars, not your peers.

TIP: The Internet lasts forever (which is why I could share the Pistorius/ Nike ad even though they took it down). Ask yourself if you'd be proud to see your current marketing photos ten years from now.

TIP: Understand that cameras are everywhere, and therefore you cannot pull off a fake or weak image for long. Live the lifestyle you are projecting and read on about narrative and authenticity before you spend a dime on image.

— 8 —

THE AGE OF THE

NARRATIVE

••••

"[Her] cutting sense of humor may not work for
most brands, but her bracing candor is part of what
Frankel's fans love about her—and what inspires
them to buy her products."

—T. L. Stanley, *AdWeek*

••••

B rash, hilarious, and honest to a fault. She is not the typical founder of a global lifestyle brand, but nothing about Bethenny Frankel is typical. Her unique communication style is precisely why her fans trust her and relate to her, allowing a strong foundation as an influencer. Her ability to turn millions of viewers into millions of consumers quite literally changed the television format, enticing networks to require a percentage of any products developed and marketed through unscripted programming.

Bethenny is a born hustler, so the risk/reward ratio of appearing on reality television didn't seem so treacherous when the opportunity arose. With a degree in psychology and communication, she understands the power of a great message. She decided the free publicity would outweigh any negative effects, so she joined the Bravo TV series *Real Housewives of New York* in its infancy to promote a book she was peddling, branding herself as a natural food chef.

As a Bravo *Real Housewife*, the unmarried, penniless Bethenny stood out among her affluent costars, with a sharp tongue that seemed unexpected at Upper East Side luncheons. Over the years, she has allowed herself to be vulnerable, sharing the best and worst aspects of her life and revealing many commonalities between her story and her audience's story. She was an ambitious, middle-aged, middle-class woman trying to become a successful businesswoman in the city. She lived in an underwhelming apartment, jumped in and out of relationships, and unapologetically maintained independence. She enjoyed fashion and entertaining, staying on a budget, and above all, cooking healthfully. Naturally, the product that shot her into the stratosphere was a low-cost, low-calorie cocktail that provided women with a healthy alternative on a fun night out.

Frankel is the millennial adaptation of the baby boomer's Martha Stewart and Generation Z's Kardashians: Her products enable middle-aged, professional women to feel empowered and successful. She created something from nothing, speaks her mind, refuses to rely on men, even taking them to the mat if needed, and demands respect. She is all about women's empowerment in business, as she is the ultimate self-made female entrepreneur. This narrative can translate to many products, the most lucrative being the global expansion of Skinnygirl.

Skinnygirl began as a one-cocktail show, a low-calorie margarita in a bottle. Seems simple enough, but this one beverage revolutionized the liquor industry and developed a subcategory of beverages marketed directly to women. The Skinnygirl product line now comprises more than 120 products including cocktail varietals, popcorn, deli meats, salad dressing, and skinny jeans, and they're all nice tie-ins to the natural chef foundation of her brand.

In addition to Skinnygirl, Bethenny offers products under her influencer brand that share the same foundational narrative. She has published self-help and recipe books, sold fan merchandise with her catchphrases, "I know it all," "Get off my jock," and others. She has enjoyed spin-off programming and a talk show executive-produced by Ellen DeGeneres, and she launched a lucrative motivational speaking career. Bethenny is also impassioned about helping underprivileged women and hurricane victims, offering immediate aid through her Bstrong foundation. And, while being successful at any one of these endeavors would be an influencer's dream, Bethenny's audience keeps rewarding her candor and relatability as she continues her ever-expanding product line.

She is a branding revolution, proving a good narrative is essential to any brand, and the product doesn't always come first.

Frankel is a textbook example of why the product component cannot fall in the center of the brand matrix. It must live harmoniously as a neighbor alongside image and narrative. In fact, in the world of reality television and instant gratification via smartphones, it is far more prevalent for the consumer to look for an appealing narrative before buying a product. Just like Skinnygirl shoppers everywhere, if the consumer likes you, they'll buy what you're selling.

THE NARRATIVE AGE

We are living in the Age of the Narrative. Every time I turn on the television some talking head is pontificating about this or that narrative, because society is beginning to realize just how powerful a 140-character tweet can be. We live in a culture of taglines, twenty-four-hour news cycles, and viral videos. A company can fail in seconds, or it can be a worldwide success in mere hours. Information is spreading like wildfire, and therefore our minds quickly process what's useful and discard the excess.

It has never been more important to understand a brand's narrative and convey it with a strong and clear message.

Many may ask, what exactly is a narrative? Well, the real answer is that *everything* is a narrative. Sounds corny? Maybe. Is it true? Yes. Literally everything and everyone around us tells a story: My Panda Planner discloses that I'm a Type A control freak and my hairstyle today lets people know I was in a rush to get out the door. Let's face it, this is my hairstyle every day, so it really says that I couldn't care less what my hair says! That's the Frankel in me, I suppose.

Have you ever sat at a gate in an airport terminal and made up stories about people and where they were going based on their choice of clothes, accessories, or luggage? Did they drag their four-year-old around on a leash? Did they look happy, sad, or anxious as hell? Are they uninterested, as if they've made this trip a thousand times before? Typically, we process these everyday narratives on a subliminal level.

Our brain subconsciously compiles the many little details, the images and actions of passersby to create a narrative that tells us who they are and what they value. For instance, if I sat across from you at the Southwest Airlines gate, you'd probably notice my wedding ring, and it would convey that I've got a better half. If you looked closer, the size or shape of my solitaire emerald-cut diamond could tell you that I favor a vintage classic style, or its size could hint at our household income. But you wouldn't know for sure. I may be sentimental; it could be a family heirloom.

As the interpreter, you create a narrative in your mind about my values, beliefs, and lifestyle based on your perceptions. Some of the story may be true, some may not, but either way, without realizing it or actively taking part in it, I have communicated many things about myself to you, a complete stranger.

EXERCISE

OBSERVING NARRATIVES

Go to a location where you feel your consumer may interact with your product. This may be a museum if you are an artist, book store if you are an author, or political rally if you are a politician. Sit down with a pen and paper for thirty minutes. Observe the people. Write down what you see. Tell their stories.

It's good to practice this type of mindfulness so you don't forget your consumer. I've been sliding through crowds at stadiums and clubs and observing the audience for years. In fact, even when I'm trying to enjoy a show off the clock, I find I'm unable to stop observing everyone around me. There's no better place to observe your consumer than when they are consuming your product.

Narratives are messages, personalities, beliefs, and values. They are the stories that are formed by our past and future lives. They are an influencer's truths, strengths, and dreams.

Narratives are the brand's identity and its purpose.

All the introspection and exercises throughout this book have been leading up to this point: You understand the importance of your own narrative and the meaning it will have to your audience and to yourself. It is imperative that you fully grasp this chapter before you attempt to define your narrative, because if you embrace a botched, fake, or weak narrative, you will not enjoy long-term success.

> **Bad Product + Bad Narrative = Failure**
>
> **Good Product + Bad Narrative = Short-term Success**
>
> **Bad Product + Good Narrative = Short-term Success**
>
> **Good Product + Good Narrative = Long-term Success**

A good narrative tells the consumer why the product is beneficial, explains how it stands out from the others, and incites an emotional response followed by a positive action. With Bethenny Frankel we have a good product and a strong narrative. Skinnygirl margarita describes a cocktail that is beneficial to the consumer because it isn't laced with sugary syrups, thereby helping reduce hangovers, both the headache kind and the gut-over-the-pants kind. The clever name stands out because it's female-focused, unlike Mike's (hard lemonade) margarita or Cayman Jack, both of which scream masculinity and calories. Skinnygirl suggests simple, fun, classy, and flirty. The imagery of the frosted glass bottle, female figurine, font choice, and red monochromatic design work together to tell the same story. Unless there is a drastic change in the product or the narrative, Skinnygirl is going to be around for a long while.

I recently witnessed an impressive *Shark Tank* pitch. Three siblings presented their deceased father's invention, the Cut Board Pro, and within hours they had a back order of over $1 million worth of product. At the same time, they raised money on GoFundMe for New York City firefighters struggling with 9/11-related illnesses. They began their pitch by sharing the unique design behind the cutting board, easily separating their product from its competitors. They finished by sharing the company's purpose, which is to honor their father's dream, stay strong as a family despite losing both their parents within a year of each other, and give back to the first responders, who, like their father, risked their lives on 9/11. Within minutes, the audience learned about a great product, as well as the company's values, beliefs, dreams, and most important, purpose.

The narrative is real, relatable, and raw. It features all three rhetorical appeals—pathos, logos, and ethos. Did I need a new cutting board? Nope. Am I on the waiting list to get the Cut Board Pro? Yep. Tens of thousands of us jumped online and sought out the product before the episode had even ended, because we wanted to help this young family achieve their purpose.

A good product with a good narrative entices the consumer to participate in the story.

When *Shark Tank*'s viewers opened their wallets and bought the product, they became part of the narrative. As long as these young entrepreneurs communicate how the consumers have helped and how they can help in the future, they will have brand-loyal customers before they know it.

BEWARE THE BAD NARRATIVE

The common misconception about bad narratives is that they are all unexpected scandals like Oscar Pistorius's murder conviction, Lance Armstrong's performance enhancers, or Tiger's infidelities and alcohol abuse. While it is true that this type of bad narrative dominates headlines and should be avoided at all costs, it is far from the only possible scenario for which an influencer should prepare.

A bad narrative can happen at any time, to anyone, in a multitude of ways. It may develop in the infancy of a brand, stunting potential growth, or years after it has been solidified in the public psyche, damaging the brand's relationship with its consumer. The impact on the brand may be localized or global, minor or extreme, forgivable or unrecoverable. It can be the influencer's doing or caused by an outside, unforeseen source. There are a multitude of bad narratives and they fall under the following categories:

- Inauthentic
- Common
- Muddled
- Insincere
- Limiting
- Misdirected
- Missing

INAUTHENTIC NARRATIVE

An inauthentic internal narrative results when a message is either conceived without regard to the influencer's private narrative, personality traits, or lifestyle choices, or when it is blatantly misleading. Inauthenticity may work for a short time, but the truth will always be revealed. A Heisman Trophy winner throws it all away with partying and extreme cockiness and ends up on a team in Canada . . . ahem . . . Johnny Manziel. When this happens, the consumer will feel betrayed and high-priced publicists on damage control will generate an apology tour, a stint at rehab, or public volunteerism. This type of bad narrative is almost always fatal to a brand, and if forgiven by the consumer, will require a complete rebrand to incorporate the new reality.

Inauthentic external narratives are assumptions made by the consumer about your brand based on current provided information. For instance, the Nashville Predators may trade or cut a player. Both moves send a negative message to the audience and other teams about the abilities of the unfortunate player. On the other end of the spectrum, a player receives a massive multiyear, multimillion-dollar contract with big headlines and then fails to live up to the inflated expectations with even bigger headlines. Overhyped brands are just as guilty of inauthenticity. The cure is to flood the marketplace with truths about the brand to drown out the wrong assumptions or information. This scenario is easily survivable.

Influencers fall prey to inauthentic narratives, both internal and external, most often, which is why it's imperative to understand how to define a successful narrative and evolve over time.

COMMON NARRATIVE

A common narrative is choosing to lead with a story that's been told before. A common narrative is boring. It's the same ole, same ole. A good narrative must include a twist that makes the message unique and interesting.

Many stories and themes do repeat themselves. For instance, my husband will say that most movies have the same plot lines as *Star Wars*: There's the battle between good and evil, the estranged parent and child, orphaned child turns into strong leader, and I could go on. Nevertheless, there's only one Luke Skywalker and Darth Vader. There's only one Death Star. These details make the oft-told story unique.

Another example is the Cinderella story. The rags-to-riches tale has been retold countless times and is a theme that continuously inspires. However, even a story that encourages goodwill toward its protagonist will fall short if there is nothing unique or interesting to elevate it above past stories.

MUDDLED NARRATIVE

A muddled narrative lacks focus. Too many diverting storylines will confuse the consumer. Many of my clients have trouble focusing their narrative to a few key topics, especially on social media. They want to change out their profile pictures every week or overshare various aspects of their lives that are not relevant. These types of impulses are very common, and very innocent.

In order to keep an engaged audience, the narrative must be streamlined. Consumers need to know what kind of information they will get when they follow a specific influencer. A good rule of thumb is to focus on no more than three to four topics. For instance, a musician may choose music, travel, and clothing topics based on his or her purpose and strengths.

Not only that, but just like adaptable design, the same message should appear on the website, social media outlets, during interviews, everywhere.

INSINCERE NARRATIVE

An insincere narrative is one that seems advantageous. Sometimes this can come from the information shared by the influencer, but often it is the delivery that makes the audience disconnect. Think of a singer crying on cue each night of their tour as they launch into the ballad, or Taylor Swift's surprised face. Cringe.

Lady Gaga received criticism during a media tour for *A Star Is Born* for repeating the same line about Bradley Cooper during every interview, word for word: "There can be one hundred people in the room and ninety-nine don't believe in you, and you just need one to believe in you, and that one was him." Google the mash-up on YouTube and give credit to Bradley Cooper for keeping a straight face. The audience, however, could not keep a straight face and turned Gaga into a punch line. The quote was manufactured and, therefore, felt insincere.

Details of a story do not matter if the influencer comes across as disingenuous. Although the example above would not constitute the dismantling of an entire career, other influencers, mainly politicians, do not get off so easily. It is best to avoid the appearance of insincerity to keep the narrative clean.

LIMITING NARRATIVE

A narrative can be limiting in both timeliness and scope. Typically, we see these issues when an influencer becomes centered on a fad. Showing appreciation for a trend is normal but becoming reliant on one can spell trouble, as the influencer will disappear just as quickly.

Politicians and online influencers need to be especially aware of this problem, as major political movements come and go as fast as a news cycle these days. The trick is to make sure the overall narrative is not so specific that it cancels out the possibility of growing or evolving.

MISDIRECTED NARRATIVE

A misdirected narrative is targeted at the wrong audience. Influencers tend to choose their target audience based on who they want their audience to be, instead of who they really are. It is imperative to look at the data and remember that no response is a response. The story can be great, unique, interesting, and honest, but if it does not incite emotion and action, the narrative has failed.

MISSING NARRATIVE

Having no narrative is the worst possible scenario. Contrary to popular belief, the product will not speak for itself. Yet, this mistake is surprisingly common. Why? An influencer will go out into the marketplace thinking, "I will use my charm to win them over. I'm pretty interesting, I can talk about anything." Charm and wit may open up a spot on *The Tonight Show* couch, but it won't keep the seat reserved for future appearances. If you don't have anything important to say, no one will listen.

Bad narratives may slither around in the grass until the camouflage fades or they may leap with a sudden strike. Many of these transgressions cannot be corrected by an apology tour, because there is nothing overt to apologize for. Therefore, it is vital for influencers to be on the alert and prepared to avoid any long-term damage that may occur from a bad narrative. Knowing how to define a unique narrative and how to communicate that message before entering the marketplace is the offense that provides the greatest defense.

TAKE CONTROL

The first thing I want to stress is that the narrator of any story has complete control over how the narrative is presented to the audience. That's great news. An influencer can decide what to reveal and what to withhold, to remain positive or negative, and to determine their role, tone, and point of view. They also decide which form (think product!) is the best to present these elements. Remember, a musical artist could use a song to showcase their story, but they could also write a book, participate on a blog, or share a behind-the-scenes video clip on YouTube. Even a television interview is fair game.

Imagine an artist, athlete, comedian, or actor making their first appearance on *The Tonight Show*. The first impression projected to the audience during a five-minute interview needs to emphasize the brand pillars. Therefore, it is industry practice to walk influencers through media training sessions. Media training demonstrates how to stay on message and pivot when necessary, how to use body language and tone to the best advantage, and how to make a story entertaining and distinctive.

From a business perspective, this preparation can eliminate the potential risk of wandering off message, which could harm a brand. But from a psychological level, I find this training invaluable, as it allows the influencer to take control over their own narrative, thereby instilling confidence and excitement. Taking ownership over a narrative makes an influencer enthusiastic about sharing their message. This energy allows a greater natural connection with the audience and creates that great first impression.

Just as important to note, however, is that the influencer does not have control over how the audience may interpret the narrative. Once that story goes out into the world, it belongs to the audience. Each person interprets the narrative in terms of their own experience, assumptions, and perceptions. A non-college-educated white female in her forties could translate the motto Make America Great Again to mean that her children will be better off with a non-politician running the White House. On the other hand, a college-educated female in her fifties who is currently the CFO of her company could ask, "Aren't we already great?" They both heard the same narrative, but each assigned it a different meaning relevant to their own identities and beliefs.

At a philosophical level, I alone can see the world in which I live, and therefore each person experiences the world in a unique way. Take any episode of *Real Housewives* as an example. The entire series is based on the exploitation of what happens when women perceive situations differently. One woman says she is worried about her friend, the other wonders why she's gossiping. One woman experiences an event completely differently than five of her closest friends. The facts are the same for each woman, like the date of the event, the people who were there, the flowers, the shrimp cocktails. But, each woman experiences the event from a slightly different point of view, and this is how each one's narrative of the same event differs.

Influencers must take complete control of their own narrative, while at the same time understanding it may be interpreted differently by their audience. Bethenny Frankel learned to share her truths, the good and the ugly, every week on television. By listening to her audience, she navigated the reality television world to learn which types of storylines she should embrace season after season, all while focusing on her Skinnygirl brand. Even as she maneuvered all the drama with her costars, she remained true to her pillars. She's a strong, independent, brash, self-made hustler. She cusses, gets drunk, ugly cries, and makes a scene just to prove she's a real person, but she wakes up the next day and rocks the CEO title. These disparate elements complete her entertaining and inspiring narrative and avoid the potential negative narratives that could arise. The audience sees that she is honest and raw. They love her for it. And then they go out and buy Skinnygirl jeans.

TWO TRUTHS AND A LIE

Let's play a game. Imagine that we just met and are about to have a brief conversation to introduce ourselves. Within that introduction, we both must include two truths and one lie about ourselves. Afterwards we both have to guess each other's lie. Get out a sheet of paper and take a few minutes to write all three supposedly truthful statements down. They can be about you, something that you did, something that happened to you, anything you want. I'll wait . . .

Okay, what were the two truths from your entire lifetime that you chose to write down? With all your experience, social interactions, family life, education, work, what did you choose to share about yourself to a perfect stranger to let them know who you are in just five minutes or less? I know for some of you this is an easy task, but for most, like me, it is daunting. The first time I did this exercise, I froze and couldn't come up with a thing. Not one. The number of life experiences I have accumulated in almost four decades seems impossible to narrow down to two brief statements. How can I communicate all that I am in just a quick, short introduction? The pressure!

Yet, this is precisely what I'm asking you to do when developing your brand narrative. Identity formation can be a bumpy ride and requires tremendous introspection. You should be thinking about all the true things about yourself you want to share and at the same time realize just how many amazing truths you have to choose from. Of course, you won't be limited to just one or two, but you will need to focus on just a few that will become core pillars.

Moving on, what lie did you tell? Did you write down a near truth for your lie by changing one insignificant point? For instance, I wrote down that I worked at Sony Music Entertainment for nine years, when I actually worked there for ten years. It's a slight variation that would easily trick a stranger. Did you write down blatant lies and rock a strong poker face? For instance, I could have shared that I went skydiving last year for my birthday. For the record, there's no chance in hell I would jump out of a perfectly good airplane and I doubt there is anything about my demeanor that would suggest I'm either reckless or an adrenaline addict.

While I was searching frantically for two revealing facts about myself, my partner was calm and collected, and I was easily manipulated by her body language. I studied her face and scrutinized everything she shared. Did she lie about where she went to college? Did she lie about where she grew up? Is she really single? I could not decipher her deceit. Once I gave up, she finally revealed that she had introduced herself as Jessica, yet her name was Sarah. BAM! Right off the bat: a small inconsequential detail! I never would have guessed she gave a fake name. So creative, and quick, and had absolutely no bearing on who she was as a person. A Jessica can easily be a Sarah.

Now, the purpose of playing this game is not to encourage you to incorporate lies in your narrative. I am never in favor of manufacturing brands in a vacuum, because authenticity is one of the most powerful elements of any narrative. My goal is for you to appreciate that **delivery and presentation are just as important as what information is shared.**

NARRATIVE MANIPULATION

Okay, so I don't embrace lying or creating a false brand identity, but there is nothing wrong with a little narrative manipulation. In order to make a brand unique and exciting, facts are often omitted or added to the narrative. Have you ever heard the phrase, "Put a spin on it"? This simply means communicate the story in a way that highlights your client's best features or selling points. I do this all the time for my celebrity artists.

The first female country artist to debut at number
one with a debut album!
The superstar artist has certified 10 million albums sold!

There are many female country artists who have debuted at number one, but my artist was the first to debut at number one with her *debut* album. I found the one minor detail that could be added to make her unique and competitive, then accented the fact to her advantage.

And, the superstar who sold 10 million albums had actually sold 10 million during the span of his entire career. In reality, his sales were trending down over the past few albums, but by omitting a reference to time, I made it seem as if the sales were recent. I did not lie, I spun it. By the way, even terms like *superstar* can manipulate a narrative. The word itself means nothing, as there are no criteria for what constitutes a superstar, yet it makes the artist seem larger than life.

A great example of how one small element in the story can be altered to project a completely different narrative is the hit NBC show *This Is Us*. The pilot episode begins with a statement claiming that the average person shares a birthday with 18 million people and that there are no known behavioral links. The audience then catches their first glimpse of the main character, Jack, as his very pregnant wife is giving him his traditional birthday lap dance with her lingerie on top of her clothes. Then viewers are introduced to the remaining three characters: a single Caucasian woman, Kate, who is obese; a wealthy African-American man, Randall, who leaves his corner office to attend a soccer game with his adoring wife and two daughters; and Kevin, the famous sitcom bachelor with an impressive six-pack.

During the next thirty minutes of the show, the audience learns that all four of the characters are turning thirty-six years old on the same day and they are all struggling with major life turning points. Kevin, after feeling belittled by the sitcom's director, has a major breakdown on set, and ultimately quits. The moment is captured by the audience's smartphones and broadcast across media outlets, leaving his career in an embarrassing limbo. Kate literally falls off her scale, and after questioning how she has found herself immensely overweight with no love life in sight, joins a support group and meets someone of interest. Randall encounters his biological father, a druggie who abandoned him at the door of a fire station decades before. He discovers that he is finally drug free, but dying of stomach cancer. And Jack's wife goes into a complicated labor and delivery with triplets and is distraught with grief when the third child is stillborn.

At the conclusion of the broadcast, Jack befriends a fireman who just dropped off an abandoned baby. Jack, mourning the loss of his third child, but determined to leave the hospital with three healthy babies, decides to adopt the orphan. At this moment, the camera view pushes outward, and for the first time, the audience sees the full scope of the hospital's waiting area: a nun in a habit, smokers in a sterile environment, bell bottoms, and a tube television broadcasting a news report about the Iran hostage crisis, all clues that Jack and his wife are living out their drama in 1980. Kate, Randall, and Kevin are their children living in present time. It isn't until the end that the viewer realizes the five strangers are in fact a family unit.

The storytellers chose which elements of the story to reveal and when to do so, yet there was no deceiving dialogue or untruths before the reveal. They strategically hid time by providing insufficient visual details. The bedroom was empty of all props except for a mattress and moving boxes, and the hospital room was bare. They used cinematic trickery because without an accurate perception of time, the audience could not distinguish vital elements of the narrative like the characters' roles, conflicts, or purpose.

That purpose, or the meaning of the story, is far more important than the details, but the details are what make it unique. On the NBC website for the show, the creators disclose the purpose: "This grounded, life-affirming dramedy reveals how the tiniest events in our lives impact who we become, and how the connections we share with each other can transcend time, distance and even death." Could another family of characters tell the same story? Could the narrative still be effective in a different setting or if it was told through a different medium like a movie? Have you ever seen *About Time* starring Bill Nighy and Rachel McAdams? Look it up, watch it, then compare the above show's purpose with the movie. They both share a common narrative but enjoy distinctive twists that create entirely new, unique narratives.

If you are going to practice narrative manipulation, be wary of crossing the line into dishonesty.

Stay away from manipulating core pillars or inflating facts.

My artist did sell 10 million albums; that fact is not contrived, nor does the number of albums sold have anything to do with his core pillars. A fake story will be uncovered faster now than it has been in the past; anyone can find out how many fake Twitter followers are lurking on an influencer's profile with one click of the mouse. Blatant deceit is not worth the risk.

THE INTERSECTION

For an influencer, the intersection of product and image is really where a narrative begins to tell a unique story. We discussed how the Skinnygirl narrative sets it apart from other alcoholic drinks in the marketplace, but how does Bethenny Frankel stand out from other television personalities? For example, what makes Frankel differ from Rachael

Ray? Both are strong female influencers who have created empires in the food and beverage industries. They are both chefs, philanthropists, and self-made businesswomen. Where do their stories diverge?

First, they have different types of products in the marketplace. One has a cooking-based talk show, one excels in the reality genre; one has cookbooks in the marketplace, the other has focused on self-help; and one offers cookware and dog food, while the other offers cocktails and jeans. Second, they have different images. One dresses for a relaxed night in, the other for a wild, upscale night out. And lastly, their personalities are polar opposites. Rachael is wholesome and welcoming with an aw-shucks persona, Bethenny is witty and strong-willed with an edge of fearlessness.

When product, image, and narrative come together, the narrative becomes stronger and clearer to both the influencer and the consumer. Influencers are able to focus on projects and outlets that advance the brand instead of wasting time and money on unhelpful ventures. Consumers are able to process, react, and purchase more quickly. There is a greater chance for long-term brand loyalty. And, the empire grows . . .

WHAT'S NEXT?

You now have a good handle on the brand matrix and how all three of its elements—product, image, and narrative—are integral parts of your influencer brand. Your understanding of narrative gives you the power to control your own story, and, by listening to the audience, understand how they may perceive it.

- Play Two Truths and a Lie with at least three people and use different truths and lies each time. Did they trick you? How did they present the information?

- Write down your five truths that best represent your purpose and strengths.
- What are four topics of expertise that you would like to focus on throughout your career? Do they play into your strengths and purpose? Do they help highlight your brand narrative?

Part 3 will dive deeper into narratives and discuss authenticity, evolution, and the power of consistency to prepare you for creating your own long-term narrative before we complete your influencer brand.

PART 3:
Boosting the Brand

— 9 —

THE TRUTH WILL
ALWAYS WIN

● ● ● ●

"Authenticity is a collection of choices that we
have to make every day. It's about the choice to
show up and be real. The choice to be honest.
The choice to let our true selves be seen."

—Brené Brown, researcher, professor, and author of
The Gifts of Imperfection

● ● ● ●

The year was 1997. The unemployment rate was low and the stock market high, continuing a trend for the next few years. This was pre–Monica Lewinsky, pre-Napster, and pre-smartphones. Steve Jobs returned to Apple, priming himself and his company for one of the greatest comebacks ever, and *Titanic* was just beginning its epic journey on the silver screen.

On a Wednesday evening in April, tens of millions of Americans gathered around their television sets to witness a reveal that had been built up to larger-than-life proportions. Just a week earlier, *Time* magazine ran a cover with a public declaration that has since been carved into American pop culture: "Yep, I'm gay!"

Ellen DeGeneres had come out of the closet, and her sitcom character on *Ellen* was about to follow suit. That night, Ellen became the first openly gay prime-time sitcom star, and America proved they weren't quite ready. The show's ratings plummeted, and major advertisers pulled their money, forcing the one-time hit comedy to crash despite critical acclaim. The comedian quickly disappeared from the spotlight, and her career was packed away in hibernation.

Then, more than five years later, the unprecedented happened. America had gone through the tremendous upheavals of 9/11, and in its aftermath, had united in a newfound sense of community. We were living in an era of *Will & Grace* and gay rights activism. And Ellen came dancing across the crisp, clean, blue-and-white set, reinvented once again, this time as a talk show host. Would the same audience who shut her out just a few years prior open their arms and minds with a friendly welcome?

PRIVATE VS. PUBLIC NARRATIVES

Ellen's life is a story of two worlds colliding, the private narrative and the public narrative. At first glance, this example seems like a cautionary tale to keep one's private life sequestered no matter the cost, but in fact that couldn't be further from reality. By keeping distance from the audience, the potential for a connection dies. And we've already discussed how an inauthentic narrative will destroy a career. The smart play now is to make sure that major elements of an influencer's private life, we'll call them defining characteristics, are seamlessly infused into the public narrative from the start.

Prominent figures cannot keep a secretive life as they used to. Tabloids and social media see to that. Within seconds, a video of Justin Bieber peeing into a restaurant's mop bucket goes viral. Even videos from the past resurface: Just ask former *Today* show personality

Billy Bush how Donald Trump's approval of sexual assault ended the former's career. He lost his good-guy reputation just for being in the room laughing along instead of chastising the reality TV star long before Trump ran for the White House. What happened to Trump in this scenario is also enlightening. We'll talk about that in a minute.

When a public brand reveals an inconsistent private narrative after the audience has bought in, people feel betrayed and react accordingly. The more support the audience has given, the greater the betrayal and the angrier the mob. The reveal dismantles the consumer's trust and leaves them feeling manipulated. Trust in every relationship is necessary, and it goes two ways, skating back and forth between influencer and consumer.

Even without a direct personal connection, there has to be complete trust between consumer and influencer.

Trust is at the confluence of celebrity and influencer. You can be famous, but without the audience's explicit trust, you cannot be an influencer.

For the record, I don't think Ellen blatantly lied to the American people. I think she was still figuring out life. Aren't we all? We are complex, layered, and constantly evolving. Trying to incorporate every element that makes someone unique and human into their brand is impossible. I'm also not advocating that everything has to be revealed. Everyone needs privacy and a sense of self outside of the spotlight. But what I am saying is all key traits must be revealed. Ellen had other characteristics that defined her brand, so why was this one element of her lifestyle so essential? How do influencers prepare now for a possible authenticity issue down the road?

The goal for any influencer should be to focus on and incorporate the elements that they consider defining characteristics. Ellen's sexual orientation is deeply rooted in who she is and what she stands for. To her, it is a defining characteristic. To her, it is of crucial import. Prior to coming out, she did not feel as if she was being her true self by hiding this one aspect of her life, to the point where it was affecting her health and happiness. Ellen felt her sexual preference was so vital to her identity that she was willing to lose everything in order to share it openly. If it is that important to the influencer and their well-being, it will be that important to the audience.

Being open and honest about who we are is what makes us unique individuals and what helps us connect with others. The original sitcom-Ellen brand was stunting her growth; she could be a celebrity, but she could not become an influencer. The original public narrative disregarded a defining characteristic. By omitting this key trait at the beginning, she robbed herself of the opportunity to fully realize her confidence and happiness, and she also robbed the audience of the opportunity to develop a personal connection.

To forge a genuine relationship with her audience, Ellen had to walk down a path of rediscovery, figuring out how to naturally infuse the new truth into a fresh brand. It is important not to confuse defining characteristics with brand pillars: The prior is a trait, and the latter is a box that holds numerous traits. Discovery is a two-step process that involves identifying the defining characteristics and then classifying them into brand pillars. Ellen spent years rebranding by incorporating her private narrative into her public narrative. The death of sitcom Ellen was inevitable. The viewers needed to witness one brand die in order to make way for the birth of a more powerful brand, more powerful because it is more authentic. On the other side of that rebrand, Ellen reached the superstar influencer status that was her destiny.

So, who is this new, more powerful Ellen? Every day when she greets her audience, she infuses them with energy and laughter. An image of sunshine and palm trees covers the set's background screen. Ellen strives to keep it light and breezy in a world that has a tendency to take humor too seriously. She pranks her guests, pokes fun at herself, and keeps her repertoire family-friendly. The party-music's lyric repeats, "Have a little fun today," and the housewife watching from her couch inhales this mantra through the screen.

Ellen is witty. She is energetic and lighthearted and steadfastly refuses to don a dress. These elements of her personality and lifestyle have carried over from the Ellen of 1997.

However, Ellen has developed a massive platform that goes beyond a comedian trying to bank a few laughs. She uses her extraordinary world stage to showcase the good in humanity by highlighting good deeds done by regular, everyday viewers. She gives back to those who give back. She closes every show with the simple yet powerful reminder: "Be kind to one another." This is the current Ellen. This is the Ellen with purpose.

Through the years, she discovered that the missing pillar in her brand was social activism. This cornerstone represents her life's purpose and it is true to her private narrative. She now addresses social inclusivity and the deep responsibility that we all have to take care of our sisters and brothers. Oprah wants us to take care of ourselves by eating healthfully and practicing meditation. Ellen wants us to take care of each other.

Ellen DeGeneres successfully rebranded and embraced her new role as a positive community leader and role model. By standing up and saying she is different, she became a beacon of light for everyone else that felt he or she was different. She doesn't fight for gay rights;

she fights for social rights. She doesn't overtly preach equality and humanity and civic duty from a pulpit every time the red light comes on, because her core product is comedy, not politics. Her job is still to make people laugh. But now her audience respects her, they believe her, and, most important, they allow her to influence them. They are bonded together in trust.

"Be kind to one another" has become a one-sentence rallying cry that creates a community of do-gooders and reminds us all to embrace inclusivity, kindness, community, laughter, and social activism—everything her new brand stands for. The audience can participate in this narrative, and it has rewarded her authenticity and honesty by making her one of the most powerful influencers on the planet.

AUTHENTICITY RULES

The influencer's goal shouldn't be to manufacture a personality that they think an audience will connect with. The goal is to accent the relatable qualities of the personality and lifestyle that already exist in order to develop an authentic connection. Without these authentic relatable qualities, an influencer's product will suffer first, followed by their narrative. If a musician doesn't live the lifestyle portrayed in their songs, how can they authentically write about it, portray it, or defend it? How can a congressman propose policies for a district if they don't live in it and don't understand the lives of their constituents?

The influencers who openly embrace their true qualities, both the good and the ugly, are the ones who connect. Kanye West, for example, accents his assertive outspoken personality as part of his brand. When he steals a microphone away from innocent, demure Taylor Swift on live television to tell the world she didn't deserve to win, or when he claims the president of the United States "doesn't care about black people" during a charity broadcast, his audience doesn't bat an eye. It's expected. The fans who accepted his behavior fifteen years ago will accept it fifteen years from now.

Let's return to Donald Trump and Billy Bush. In that instance, only one brand was damaged, because only one brand was exposed as inauthentic. Those eager campaign aides that released the secret audio hoping that Trump would get bad traction apparently hadn't heard prior statements made in countless other public settings. Trump based his brand on the pillars of provocativeness, extreme opulence, and ultramasculine behavior for decades before he decided to run for president. The public, therefore, was less than shocked when the tape leaked. Trump emerged unscathed, and he went on to become the leader of our country. Billy Bush, on the other hand, had built his brand around the clean-cut, all-American, boy-next-door image. Though it was minor, the audience couldn't reconcile his part in the conversation with his brand. NBC canceled his contract for offenses under his morality clause. Bush has yet to recover.

Authenticity is not just necessary in order to stave off brand failure; it actually makes brands stronger, much stronger. Influencers who display vulnerability through their private narratives, sharing insecurities, missteps, or struggles, may reap even greater rewards as the audience develops an intense appreciation for the trust laid at their feet. It creates unbridled passion for the influencer and has even been known to start social movements.

When Meghan Trainor publicly pulled a music video because her waistline was digitally edited, she embraced her imperfections and doubled down on her public narrative, encouraging self-confidence in her audience. This narrative had been a pillar of her brand since her breakout hit, "All About That Bass," where she sings about being beautiful regardless of size and shames magazines for the use of Photoshop.

By publicly calling for the removal of the digital edits, which I'm sure got someone fired, she highlighted this brand pillar. Her audience became even more enamored with her and her war against women's negative body issues. Meghan was proving that she stood for something important. If she hadn't been vocal about her edited waistline, and the audience found out, she would have been deemed a fraud and, as a relatively new brand, she wouldn't have survived the fallout.

There are many other examples of influencers embracing their vulnerabilities publicly, while fans overwhelmingly respond with support: Owen Wilson and depression, Demi Lovato and addiction, Chrissy Teigen and infertility, Mark Wahlberg and his criminal past, Melissa McCarthy and her weight, and the list goes on. The more vulnerable these stars are with their private lives, the more the audience responds with respect and encouragement. Why? The audience shares the same struggles. They can relate. They know the influencers are being authentic.

Do not read this as permission to overshare.

**There is a fine line between being honest
and being opportunistic.**

There's also a subtle dance that influencers must do to maintain an air of mystery. So read this as permission to disregard fear and lean in. I'm a firm believer that honesty is the best policy, and it is always better for the new information to come from the influencer and not from the press. Be prepared, however, that once a new private narrative is revealed to the public, no matter how important or irrelevant, your brand will need to incorporate that new truth going forward.

Country music icon Martina McBride was already a superstar when I first started working with her. She was a mother of three and a homemaker, and she was still the fun and energetic entertainer who had burst onto the music scene almost two decades earlier with flirty and lighthearted tunes like "My Baby Loves Me." She is by far one of the best vocalists I have ever worked with, and one of the most enjoyable, and I simply adore her.

Martina's private narrative began to evolve from her original brand as she grew more and more into her role as a wife and mother. She began to release songs like "Blessed," "Happy Girl," "Broken Wing," and "Concrete Angel." Inspiration, defense of vulnerable women and children, and happy homes with Christian values were themes that made a positive impact on her existing product. These songs became some of her biggest sellers. Her private narrative had found its way into the product naturally and the new brand resonated with her audience. There was no going back.

I'm not sure if it was a conscious decision, but years later Martina wanted to resume focus on her original carefree music, presenting a younger mind-set. The lyrics were lighthearted and fun, which was always a staple, but subtracted the overt family values and Christian themes. The product didn't ring authentic, and the marketplace reacted accordingly. Luckily, she failed fast and quickly returned to embracing her authentic private narrative with yearly Christmas tours, yummy cookbooks, and a cooking show on Food Network called *Martina's Table*. If you haven't watched it yet, give it a go. She's delightful.

HILLARY'S MISSTEPS

Following the presidential campaign of 2016, stunned political pundits lamented how the qualified and poised Hillary Clinton lost to the inexperienced and unruly Donald Trump. Clinton's email servers were discussed ad nauseam. Benghazi lingered. Finally, Russian collusion slowly became the focus of conversation and the blame was cast. The truth, however, is that the main culprit was not an outside nefarious source trying to rig our election. Though that may be a potential problem for our country, it was not what lost Hillary the election. Hillary had an authenticity problem that stemmed from a decades-long career in the public eye.

Hillary's policies and qualifications, the product she was selling, were standard Democratic fare, nothing spectacular that would ruffle any feathers. In fact, policies all but disappeared from the national conversation in 2016 because they were so ordinary. Few balked at her positions. She had an impressive background with a law degree, two terms as the First Lady of the United States, two terms as a senator from New York, and one term as the US secretary of state. Few argued her qualifications.

As soon as the 2016 campaign kicked off, however, pollsters released data showing that only 12 percent of Americans thought Clinton was honest and trustworthy, and a whopping 70 percent believed she was dishonest. These dismal numbers remained relatively consistent throughout the campaign, and, by election day, Clinton was unable to cure her inauthenticity issues. Americans didn't vote for Trump because he was qualified or because he was more popular, they voted for Trump because they didn't trust Clinton.

Hillary first became a household name almost twenty-five years ago, when she was the wife of presidential hopeful Bill Clinton. Back in 1992 Bill was branded as a man of middle America. He was the aw-shucks, jeans and baseball cap, Arkansas-raised, McDonald's-loving American. His slogan was "For People, For a Change". Bill was charismatic, charming, and salt of the earth, complete with a thick Southern drawl.

This brand identity became Hillary's by transference. As the politician's wife, her duty was to project the same pillars as her husband and share the same narrative. Her moves were calculated for *his* candidacy, for his brand. In the formative years of her career, when she should have had her own brand to protect and evolve, she came up under the umbrella of his brand. The public viewed her as middle American by association, before they truly got to know her. The Clintons were one and the same. This was her first problem.

Then she left the White House and ran for the Senate. Nobody has ever done that. For presidents, two terms mark the end of the road; they cannot spend another four years in office due to constitutional restrictions, and serving in the US Congress would be a demotion. But, imagine if Bush or Obama had run for a senate seat in the state of New York once leaving the White House. Their roles as presidents, the daily scrutiny of the job, the successes and failures, and everything they stood for would haunt their candidacies like banshees. Would President Obama still be able to play the role of the selfless community organizer after he ran the free world? No. And this led to Hillary's second big problem.

Hillary faced the same challenges an ex-president does, and then some. As she embarked on a solo political career post–White House, she failed to rebrand herself by shedding her husband's past and policies, and this left her vulnerable. She did not take the time to create an individual brand, with her personalized private narrative. Consequently the public had no image, no narrative, no product separate from Bill Clinton to connect with. Who is *she*? What does *she* stand for? Having no clear brand herself means having no clear motives or purpose.

This was the root of many negative storylines that plagued the campaign. First, some voters assumed she would vote in line with her husband or that he was behind the scenes pulling the strings. Whatever he did in office, she would do the same. Whoever he promised favors to, she would follow up. She was seen as a follower, not a leader. It was the same story with Obama. Was he going to continue his policies through her? Was she just his pawn?

Second, and this is not in order of importance, her pantsuit became a story. An influencer should not allow image to take center stage in a narrative. Yet, the pantsuit was a topic that would not die. She is on the record saying that the pantsuits were a feminist tool she used to level the playing field in Congress; it allowed her to avoid embarrassing paparazzi shots up her skirt, and it took the conversation off her looks and kept it on the policies. Except, it didn't. Each time the media discussed her pantsuits, it took time and attention away from her story and her policies.

More damaging however, is that without a complete rebrand, voters were constantly, inadvertently, and subliminally reminded of her role and actions during Bill's presidency. She couldn't shake the woman who stood by her man during a *60 Minutes* interview:

> "You know, I'm not sitting here, some little woman standing by my man like Tammy Wynette. I'm sitting here because I love him, and I respect him, and I honor what he's been through and what we've been through together. And you know, if that's not enough for people, then heck—don't vote for him."

Notice the obvious undertones of the middle America brand? A bold reference to country icon Tammy Wynette and a sly "heck" thrown in for good measure? Remember, they presented themselves as one and the same. But I digress.

Her 2016 campaign platform seemed to conflict with her previous actions, creating an inauthentic narrative. She wanted to protect women's rights and herald feminism, yet she aided in the destruction of lowly intern and sexual-harassment victim Monica Lewinsky. The voters did not forget Hillary's complacency and they held her accountable for Bill's sexual harassments, rape allegations, and his subsequent congressional impeachment.

It may have helped Bill's career to have his wife by his side as a character witness, which of course was by design, but Hillary would never recover. Every scandal that wounded Bill left Hillary with a permanent scar. For American voters, the underlying narrative of that *60 Minutes* interview in 1992 was not that Bill was innocent, but that they were both more interested in capturing the White House than in atonement for his misdeeds. Without separating herself from her husband and without creating a clear brand, Hillary left the American voters to create their own, less-flattering narrative. Many came to see her as power hungry, hypocritical, and deceitful.

The shared identity with her husband was just the beginning of the dismantled trust between Hillary and voters. The apparent discord between her private and public narratives quickly went beyond mere confusion and into the realm of phoniness. She had failed to acknowledge that her lifestyle and image had changed in the years she spent in public life. She had traveled the world, entered the history books, and enjoyed both power and money. She was no longer middle America, yet she held on to that narrative because it got her husband elected. This was her second problem.

The name Clinton was an asset at first. However, by the 2016 presidential campaign, the disconnect was palpable. As first lady, she had concentrated on universal health care, the Violence Against

Women Act, and the Adoption and Safe Families Act. In Congress, she fought for federal aid to help New York rebuild after 9/11, including health care coverage for first responders. She also worked to grant full military health benefits to the National Guard. Under Obama, Secretary of State Hillary Clinton pushed for sanctions on Iran and helped negotiate the Paris Agreement on climate change. She will go down in history as being instrumental in taking out Osama bin Laden. These should be positives, but Hillary chose to hang on to Bill's middle-America narrative instead of embracing her powerful role as a world leader.

The clashing private and public narratives were further accented by the campaign's decision to push the old Clinton narrative using slogans and press stories that seemed downright disingenuous. Hillary was no longer a layman, so slogans like Stronger Together and Fighting for Us could be viewed as ironic condescension and insincere. (I guess it depends upon what the meaning of the word "us" is.) To combat editorials describing a distant, cold, and serious Clinton compared to the friendly and informal Trump, they pressed a common narrative to make her seem more loving and sympathetic: *She's just like you. Look. She's a grandmother.* This was a transparent tactic to capture female voters.

The public rebelled: *No, she's not just like me, and no, I don't care that she's a grandmother.* In fact, the entire thought process behind the grandmother messaging is an enigma. Pantsuit Hillary playing with a toddler on the living room floor, regardless of how forced and awkward the imagery, is not what the American people need from a future commander in chief. I can promise you no other presidential candidate won because they were a grandfather.

From the second Hillary decided to run for the Senate in New

York, she should have embarked on a journey to rebrand. Rebrands are never easy. They often fail, and this one, if successful, would have been a first of its kind in the political realm. It might not even have been possible to remove herself from her husband's shadow, but she certainly could have distanced herself and embraced her own, true, private narrative.

Hillary's campaign tried to pivot and deny with an inauthentic and insincere narrative: *She's not power hungry. You should see her when she's playing with her granddaughter. She's so sweet and loving.* In response to the accusation that Hillary was power hungry, the campaign could have spun power hungry into a positive and doubled down on an authentic message: *Damn right she's a strong, powerful woman who put herself through law school, and did X, Y, and Z. Now she's going to break the glass ceiling as America's first female president.* This narrative supports her independence and achievements, but more importantly it rings true.

Hillary is a prime example of how an influencer can lose control over their own narrative. By beginning her career without a narrative, then embracing an inauthentic and muddled narrative, she let the press and the American people define her brand, instead of the other way around. Once the public witnessed these subtle disconnects from Hillary's private life, the news media latched on to evidence of her hypocrisy with a vengeance. She became an easy target: *She has a private email server, she must be hiding something.* These taunts labeled her dishonest, even though other secretaries of state had their own servers too. If the campaign had embraced the new powerful, independent Hillary, and accented her attributes in a positive way to create a fresh and bold, more authentic brand, who knows? She just might have broken that stubborn glass ceiling.

WHAT'S NEXT?

Being a public figure will bring extra scrutiny to your private life and potentially create opportunities for your competition, or your audience, to poke holes in your brand. By truly living your brand, you reduce the need to constantly be on guard, freeing up energy that will be better spent on your business.

- Make a list of your defining characteristics and decide which ones must be incorporated into your brand.
- Do you have any vulnerabilities or imperfections that you would like to incorporate into your brand? Why? Ask yourself if highlighting those specific elements would help you achieve your purpose.
- Try to identify the bad narratives from Hillary's campaign. Inauthentic, muddled, insincere, common, and no narratives are all in there somewhere. Most occur a few times, so you may have quite the list. If you can spot them in her failed campaign, it'll be easier to spot them before you establish your own brand.
- Ask yourself which areas of your life you would like to keep private. Now, imagine you are already successful. Is it going to be possible to do so? Will it alter your brand or offend your audience if it is revealed?

-10-

THE RULES OF EVOLUTION

●●●●

"I have always been on the lookout for the most practical,
appealing, efficient, and sensible way to accomplish
everyday and meaningful tasks, and I have devoted my
life to discovering and sharing those solutions. Once
I find the smartest way to vacuum a room, the most
sensible way to plant a tree, the finest way to organize
a drawer, or the most beautiful way to decorate a cake,
I am committed to teaching that method until I learn
another, better way to do such a task. And I am always
aware there might be a better way!"

—Martha Stewart, the OG lifestyle influencer, in
The Martha Manual: How to Do (Almost) Everything

●●●●

Martha Stewart is the epitome of the macro-influencer. Over
the course of fifty years, she has transformed a small catering
company into an influencer's dream, a full-fledged multimedia
corporation, whose only rival is Oprah's Harpo. This feat can only
be accomplished by an influencer who has remained authentic in
her message, consistent with her pillars, and committed to growth
and evolution. As one of the first lifestyle influencers, if not the first,

Martha had to navigate the essential branding principles discussed in this book before they were principles.

She understands that she and her brand are synonymous. She understands she must connect with her audience by super-serving authentic content before asking them to make a purchase (media first, merchandise second). And she understands the importance of becoming an expert on any given topic. She even remained optimistic through adversity, saving Martha Stewart Living Omnimedia and her brand after a potentially career-ending stint in prison for insider trading. But she may be the best representative among her peers for her ability to maintain focus on her core pillars of home and everyday living while allowing the company the flexibility required to adapt and grow.

The battle between the need for consistency and the basic desire for evolution can finally rest: The truth is you need both. Martha's content does not change, nor do her values or lifestyle. Whether she's writing a book or developing a new product for Macy's, she remains dedicated to topics relating to her core themes, which are gardening, cooking, entertaining, crafting, and home decor. After decades in the public eye, her narrative continues to be about helping those interested in the home learn how to maintain and elevate it.

Alongside an overriding desire to expand her empire, Martha has an insatiable appetite for learning and creativity. She's constantly offering new content and products to her core audience. Growth and evolution are not merely traits shared by macro-influencers; they are requirements to become so. Therefore, learning how to evolve without alienating the core consumer and harming the brand should be of utmost importance to all influencers.

FLEXIBILITY AND DIVERSITY

The marketplace can change without much warning, usually due to technology, but also due to cultural and societal shifts. Outside threats and competition can wreak havoc on a company's bottom line. Even consumer complacency toward an aging brand can spell disaster. Influencers who remain flexible in their strategy and diversified in their offerings protect their business while at the same time guaranteeing constant brand rejuvenation.

Having the foresight to listen to environmental conditions, consumer behavior, and competition, as well as their own personal transformations, an influencer may not only save their brand from ruin; they could help it expand with new momentum while everyone else remains behind. If Taylor Swift hadn't embraced streaming technology, she would have become a relic. If Oprah had remained steadfast in pursuing a news anchor career, she wouldn't have become a media mogul. By conducting business with an attentive, open, and creative mind-set, these influencers were able to shift their business goals, allowing for a positive evolution for their brands.

An influencer can further protect their brand's future by building a robust portfolio of products alongside an equally varied marketing plan. Think about a retirement fund. If an investor puts all their eggs in one basket, they could lose every cent. One artist I know spent hours and hours perfecting online videos on the social network Vine. He amassed quite a large following and surpassed his fellow artists in utilizing the platform. A year later, Vine suffered a tragic death, like many social networks before it, and dragged my friend's career along with it to the grave. This could have been avoided if this artist had spent resources marketing these videos to other platforms as well.

Martha Stewart diversifies her brand by amassing a large arsenal of helpful products and innovative partnerships. In 1997, she joined forces with Kmart in a merchandising deal that was lucrative for the Martha Stewart brand. As is the case with most partnerships, this union could not last forever. Knowing this, and seeking to protect her brand, Martha entered into many partnerships in the decade that followed. Kmart has all but faded, but with her merchandise now available at Lowe's, the Home Depot, Macy's, Michaels, and J. C. Penney, Martha Stewart Living Omnimedia thrives. The brand is diversified, prosperous, and secure.

While evolution and expansion are essential to the growth of any business, an influencer must take into account how doing so may affect their brand. Each time a partnership is formed, each time a new product is created, each time a new goal is added to the business plan, decisions must be based on the brand pillars. If they don't coincide, it is not the right way to grow. If, however, a slight shift in the matrix is needed in order to aid in the brand's progression while maintaining authenticity, follow the three simple rules of evolution to maintain the brand identity.

THE RULES OF EVOLUTION

Rule #1: Make sure you have a solid foundation before a product-line or brand extension.

Martha Stewart started a catering company in the 1970s, but she didn't publish her first cookbook, *Entertaining*, until 1982. She spent almost a decade growing her main product, the catering company, becoming an expert in cooking and hosting before she expanded into publishing. Then, when she did, that new product was purely a representation of the first.

The consumer must know an influencer brand thoroughly before they become brand loyal enough to buy multiple products. They must believe in the expertise and must trust in the narrative. An influencer who comes out of the gate with multiple products creates a muddled narrative and risks the vitality of each product. Marketing resources are split, as is focus.

Stewart spent time and effort developing each new offering into a stand-alone powerhouse. The expansion was deliberate and calculated. It wasn't until the early 1990s, after many books had been released, that Stewart became editor-in-chief of *Martha Stewart Living* magazine. Nearly another decade passed before she began developing merchandising partnerships with retailers. This slow growth enables each commodity to gain its independent footing and protects the overall brand. If one fails, the rest of the house still stands.

Today, Martha Stewart has released something like ninety books. She publishes several magazines, produces television and radio programming, and continues to grow her merchandise and online assets. She has had plenty of product failures along the way, but by remaining steadfast in her pillars and meticulous in expansion, her brand will continue to serve as a solid foundation.

Rule #2: Anything about the influencer can change. Anything, that is, except the core pillars.

Pink doesn't always have pink hair, yet she remains rebellious. Taylor Swift no longer wears sundresses with cowgirl boots, yet she is still the girl next door. All brands must transform over time or they will become irrelevant. To prevent potentially damaging a brand, we look to all those ancillary descriptions and traits, the other bits that may fall around the center of the Venn diagram, as fair game.

Macro-influencers will reach multiple stages in their careers, when they will need to revive a stale brand and reach new audiences to develop new customers. A stagnant brand needs an infusion of new life, possibly incorporating a fresh and modern narrative or updating an outdated look, and a brand must always look to a new audience to add to its core base. For instance, Martha Stewart updated all her logos and visual branding in the late 2000s to liven up an aging brand, and she is consistently offering additional products to reach new consumers.

Martha turned heads when she teamed up with Snoop Dogg for a VH1 cooking show. The unlikely pair didn't share much other than being two macro-influencers in the later stages of their careers, yet the vehicle successfully introduced Martha to a new and younger audience without alienating her core base. Such a move could be deemed risky, but it's riskier to remain stationary.

Just like our imaginary Beyoncé commercial, Martha stayed true to her core pillars. It is a cooking show, after all. But she found a partner outside of the brand's normal purview, which infused it with a breath of fresh air and extended the life of an already long-standing career. Like Martha, influencers who are constantly learning and creating new ways to showcase their brand will eventually enjoy icon status.

Rule #3: Major tweaks to a brand should be made slowly over a significant period.

Each time a project is released into the marketplace, regardless of whether it is an icon or a new influencer, it is important to analyze the brand and check for any potential issues. Asking if the marketplace or the influencer's private narrative have transformed since the last release allows for a small course correction that the audience may not notice.

These minor modifications over time enable an influencer's career to progress, and sometimes repair, without requiring a rebrand.

In psychology, the threshold of change that a consumer does or does not notice is called the just noticeable difference or JND. If a cereal manufacturer wants to increase profits without losing shoppers, they may increase the price by a few cents and decrease the size of the box by a small margin. Both changes are too minor for the consumer to notice, but they make a substantial impact on the company's growth. If, on the other hand, that manufacturer wants to call attention to their organic ingredients, they may tout that selling point by adding a prominent graphic in the cover design. A small banner may not cross the threshold, but a substantial call-out would.

The goal for an influencer is to make most brand changes just below the threshold so the consumer isn't conscious of it. Noticeable tweaks, like a brand refresh, should be spaced out over a long period of time. Google "Pepsi Logo Evolution" and observe how the iconic logo evolved over 100 years from 1898 to 2011.

The evolution is like a long staircase; minor steps along the way create a major difference a century later. The first and last logo are nothing alike, but if we look at the small steps between each update, we see how subtly the brand has evolved. If Pepsi had jumped from the first to the last image, the brand's loyal customers wouldn't recognize the product on store shelves.

Look how the minor elements evolve to create major change. The same red cursive font sticks around for the first sixty years. When the company first introduced the bottle cap with the red, white, and blue motif, they kept the familiar script. It wasn't until the next revision a decade later that they changed the font and dropped the word cola.

And, notice how they transformed the curved underline from the original logo into the interior white tilde, which has remained in the circle since its first appearance on the bottle cap in the 1950s.

Pepsi was methodical with its image renovations, looking at the marketplace and the consumer's behavior each step of the way. This is a wonderful reminder to evolve all three elements of the brand—product, image, and narrative—at an almost glacial pace. Whether an influencer dances below the JND threshold or above it, acknowledging the need for growth and developing an appropriate long-term strategy to avoid a sudden rebrand is crucial to a brand's sustainability.

REBRANDING

The Walt Disney Company is a national icon that has made it almost 100 years without a major rebrand. Through peaks and valleys and a slow evolution, it has remained a vibrant part of the American culture. Disney is wholesome, friendly, and inviting. It's nostalgia for adults and wonderment for the kiddos. It's magic and imagination. There is always a happy ending at Disney. Except for its teen stars.

Teen stars have notoriously experienced a rough road transitioning their overhyped brands from childhood to adulthood, so we cannot blame Disney entirely. One day these young entertainers are making millions of dollars and the next they cannot even get an appointment with a casting director. Taylor Swift aside, most end up in the tabloids, in rehab, or worse.

When a young influencer goes from preteen to adult, the change is drastic and sudden. They are not afforded the opportunity to gradually evolve like a Pepsi logo and they do not get a smooth transition. Their worldview expands overnight, and they begin to question preconceived notions. Just like typical teenagers everywhere, they rebel. But unlike typical teens, they rebel against corporately molded identities in order to harness control and independence over their future selves. They reassess priorities, maybe discover a minor trait as a defining characteristic, and often flounder trying to develop a new lifelong purpose. In essence, they are at the stage of life when they discover who they really are. This is a precarious time for any teenager, let alone those in the public eye.

Daniel Radcliffe, the young actor who portrayed Harry Potter, left his fanciful sorcery days for amplified adult roles requiring nudity in the art world's more respectable theater scene. Adorable Elijah Wood went from cutesy *Flipper* costar to the epic *Lord of the Rings* trilogy. Mayim Bialik became famous in the sitcom *Blossom* in the '90s. She then went on to earn a PhD in neuroscience before returning to television to play a neuroscientist on *The Big Bang Theory*. Miley Cyrus left Disney's *Hannah Montana* to swing naked in "Wrecking Ball" and twerk on Robin Thicke.

All of these young actors grew into adults with more complex private narratives. They are shedding their old selves and their old brand and reemerging in new skin. This is not a mere tweak to a small portion of our matrix because all three main elements of the brand (product, image, and narrative) will be affected when core pillars are changed. Without a complete rebrand, the influencer will develop dissonance within these elements, causing inauthenticity. An attempt to rebrand is the only way to survive.

Here's the catch: The stronger the initial brand, the harder it is for an influencer to disassociate themselves from that brand. When the public sees a paparazzi image of Miley Cyrus smoking pot, the reaction is shock, dismay, and disappointment. Subconsciously they are yelling, "Hannah Montana wouldn't do that!" Hannah was the massive star, and the real Miley came second. If Miley hadn't been wildly successful as her lead character and had instead entered the music industry as a female rocker, those same consumers wouldn't even bat an eye. Rock and roll is synonymous with sex and drugs. The behavior is expected.

To make matters worse for Miley, her initial brand was not only deeply associated with the safe-for-the-whole-family Hannah Montana, she was also associated with a much stronger brand, the Walt Disney Company. The Disney brand is so dominant and far reaching that its core pillars are immediately transferred to any young actors or musicians associated with the company. This powerful halo effect is exactly why a young novice would want to be associated with the company in the first place. With Disney's strong brand loyalty, and high brand equity, Hannah Montana was all but sure to be a huge hit.

Yet, as Miley grew up looking to capitalize on her strong Hollywood start, she ended up facing a brand crisis. She needed to demonstrate independence and power. She needed to disassociate herself from Hannah Montana and from Disney. She needed to incorporate her new life into her new brand. And, she did all this with a massive jolt.

Thanks to a raunchy VMA performance, her audience was thrown off balance, the Internet exploded, and overnight, Miley was no longer associated with her Disney character. Not all influencers need such a drastic shake-up, but she wanted an extreme variance to make a point. And make a point she did.

The reaction that followed helped the starlet redefine her purpose and focus her public efforts to support the LGBTQ and homeless communities. Miley discussed the aftermath with *People* magazine: "It inspired me to use my platform for something much bigger. If the world is going to focus on me and what I am doing, then what I am doing should be impactful and it should be great." She has since mellowed out and found a place somewhere between "Party in the USA" and Robin Thicke's legs.

Obviously a rebrand is not a guarantee of future success. It typically costs double the initial brand and requires much more effort.

The only reason to rebrand is if there are no other options.

Miley took a huge risk, but she had nothing to lose. Either way, she had grown out of her initial brand and needed to move forward.

The best way to ensure a successful rebrand is by putting the product 100 percent front and center. Taking time to make the best new product possible will encourage open-mindedness in the consumers, enabling them to appreciate the new image and narrative and inciting a positive reaction. Remember, a positive/neutral first impression leads to the possibility of a positive lasting impression, and a negative first impression is hard to remedy. If a new product fails, the new narrative or image won't matter, as the consumer will brush it aside as flailing antics. If, for instance, the album *Bangerz*, featuring the hits "We Can't Stop" and "Wrecking Ball," hadn't received rave reviews from critics and sold millions, Miley's rebrand would have been thwarted and her attempt would have become a punch line.

Rebrands are not reserved for those going through puberty, although these types of rebrands are so drastic that they are a good illustration of the potential problems. The need for a rebrand may arise at any time in an influencer's career. Lady Gaga is one of the best-selling artists in history, but she has seen album sales plummet since her debut. Her platform, built on a gimmick that was overly focused on meat dresses and egg-pod entrances, could not be sustained over the long term.

As her record sales dropped from 15 million to 6 million to a dismal 1 million, Gaga's career hit a wall and her brand needed a reboot.

The intense focus on image threw off the delicate balance within the matrix. She parted ways with her manager and refocused on what she does well: She played multiple characters. She jumped into acting head first, winning a Golden Globe for her role in *American Horror Story* and an Oscar nomination for megahit *A Star Is Born*. She ended up winning the Oscar for Best Original Song, helping to cement a new brand she had been working toward for years.

Lady Gaga is no longer the outlandish outsider with bewildering interviews and extravagant red-carpet appearances. She is now poised, articulate, and prefers haute couture over face paint, green wigs, and skin-tight latex. There's still a touch of inauthenticity surrounding the brand, as her message sometimes feels prepackaged, but at least people are talking about her product rather than discussing her antics. That's an upgrade.

How do you know whether you may need to tackle a rebrand? An influencer only gets one chance at a rebrand, so you'd better be sure. A weak brand can get stronger over time, and a confusing brand can become clearer. Ask yourself the following questions and if you respond yes to any situation that cannot be remedied slowly over time, you may need to invest in a rebrand.

- Did your life priorities radically change since the release of your first project? (i.e.: did you get married, have a baby, realize the earth was round?)
- Did your purpose change?
- Do you need to incorporate a new defining characteristic? Remember, Ellen had to rebrand!
- Did two or more of your core pillars change, thereby throwing off the authenticity of your brand elements: product, image,

and narrative? If only one changed, you may get away with a slow evolution.

- Do you have a bad narrative associated with your brand, one that struck suddenly or developed over time? Could it be time for a positive refresh?
- Are the consumers responding negatively to your brand? Don't forget, no response is still a response.
- Was your original brand too closely associated with a more powerful brand?
- Is your brand unique, or did you develop your brand on the back of another?
- Are you Hillary Clinton?

WHAT'S NEXT?

You've made it through the wilderness. Somehow, you've made it through. You've learned how to build a brand matrix, and you understand how authenticity, consistency, and evolution are keys to creating and maintaining a successful influencer brand. You are officially ready for your own brand identity formation. That's right! It's time to gather all your notes from the previous chapters, ask yourself some tough questions, and turn your brand into a personalized mission statement. Flip to the next page to begin developing your brand!

—11—

LEAN IN

••••

"You are entering a different business world than I entered. Mine was just starting to get connected. Yours is hyperconnected. Mine was competitive. Yours is way more competitive. Mine moved quickly, yours moves even more quickly. As traditional structures are breaking down, leadership has to evolve as well. From hierarchy to shared responsibility, from command and control to listening and guiding . . . you'll have to rely on what you know. Your strength will not come from your place on some org chart; your strength will come from building trust and earning respect. You're going to need talent, skill, and imagination and vision, but more than anything else, you're going to need the ability to communicate authentically, to speak so that you inspire the people around you, and to listen so that you continue to learn each and every day on the job."

—Sheryl Sandberg, COO, Facebook,
Harvard Business School commencement speech, 2012

••••

Throughout my many years working with influencers at all levels of their careers, I have never, not once, met someone who stumbled into a successful brand. They do not—Sheryl Sandberg included—wake up one day blessed with the ability to communicate authentically or to inspire others. They do not suddenly know how to brand themselves or stay true to that brand over the course of a career. These are skills that take time and effort. Those who are thriving have worked long and hard to find their purpose, to develop a strong product, image, and narrative, and to build a viable business from scratch.

Sandberg was thirty-eight years old before beginning her tenure at Facebook, and she was forty-three years old before publishing her first book, *Lean In: Women, Work, and the Will to Lead*, a manifesto for women's rights in the workplace. She spent twenty years, if not more, developing an expertise in economics and tech and her reputation as a strong leader in an industry lacking female power. Years into her career, she identified a need in the marketplace and solidified her purpose to inspire other businesswomen.

Do you think Sandberg was able to foresee such an incredible career trajectory as a young graduate? As she says herself, the world is different today than it was when she left Harvard Business School. Silicon Valley hadn't even been born. She made lateral moves and vertical moves, crossed industries, and eventually found her powerful voice on arguably the most powerful platform ever created.

Every career has a beginning, and every career an end. Most may think a typical influencer's career looks like a bell curve: a sluggish start, a surge in power and awareness, a climactic crescendo, and then a slow burnout before a final disappearance. This is not realistic. This does not account for the many peaks and valleys that a brand naturally encounters. A career trajectory, therefore, will look more like this:

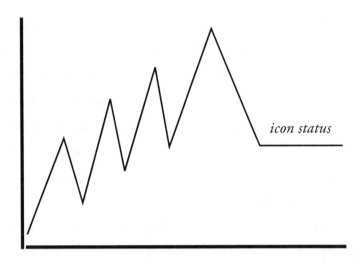

icon status

This is a fairly accurate depiction of a long and prosperous career with ups, downs, and slow upward momentum. We shouldn't fear these peaks and valleys. Instead we ought to welcome them and use them to our advantage. In fact, each peak must be followed by a cooling-off period, lest the influencer overwhelm the marketplace, creating a surplus of supply with dwindling demand.

Justin Timberlake rides these waves, leaving four years or more between each album release. During his downward slopes, he concentrates on other creative endeavors that enable him to preserve a healthy dose of public visibility. His brand stays relevant, he nurtures his passions, and he enjoys creative freedom, all while building up consumer demand for his music and ensuring a higher peak at his next product launch.

Want to hear the best part? Since Timberlake is in no rush to release his latest and greatest like other musicians, who release an album every year to avoid the valleys, he can devote ample time and energy into creating high-quality products. He is winning on multiple fronts, all by embracing the slowdowns.

Notice that the troughs should never return to the line of oblivion. Timberlake is always evolving. He never disappears completely. By recognizing a valley on the horizon, an influencer can prepare for a new offering or a slight brand update and embark on a growth pattern to avoid the need for a full comeback situation. If an influencer works hard enough at evolving their brand, they will not only ensure that the low points never reach the bottom, they will also capture elusive icon status.

Icons are the influencers we still talk about fifty or more years after their passing. They are the ones whose estates make millions of dollars until the copyrights expire, or the ones who we learn about in history books. An influencer who reaches icon status makes it over their last peak, then plateaus somewhere in the middle. The rate of the final decrescendo depends on how influential they were in life. Einstein passed in the 1950s, John Kennedy in the 1960s, Elvis Presley in the 1970s. These are all icons we continue to celebrate. Will society still honor these powerful figures 100 years from now? It's certainly possible. Aristotle is still persuasive more than 2,000 years later.

Now, each influencer is going to have wildly different trajectories. Whatever path your career may take, a business and an audience takes time to develop. It takes time to practice, it takes time to discover your brand, and it takes time to grow. Your first attempt at establishing your brand will be a rough draft. Stick with it. Just remember to listen to your consumers, fail fast, and most important, **stay true to yourself, and you will stay true to your brand.**

THE FLYWHEEL EFFECT

The beginning may seem like a difficult place to start, but it's the easiest. Spend the time to get to know yourself and your brand. Do the exercises in this book multiple times if necessary. Taking these deliberate steps to create a lasting brand identity will allow for a marketing strategy that is efficient, and more important, effective. Without that effort now, you risk everything later, as each strategy in place will push you further and compound to create a stronger, longer-lasting brand.

I liken it to the Flywheel Effect as laid out in *Good to Great: Why Some Companies Make the Leap . . . and Others Don't* by the well-known business management consultant Jim Collins. You push the massive wheel forward, inch by inch, apply more effort, push faster, and eventually the heavy wheel propels forward sustained by its own momentum. The more work done now, the better off you are in the future. Collins writes:

> "Each turn of the flywheel builds upon work done earlier, compounding your investment of effort . . . Now suppose someone came along and asked, 'What was the one big push that caused this thing to go so fast?' You wouldn't be able to answer; it's just a nonsensical question. Was it the first push? The second? The fifth? The hundredth? No! It was all of them added together in an overall accumulation of effort applied in a consistent direction."

It is tough to get the wheel moving. No one will deny this. But with all that pushing, there will come a day, after countless hours of practice and preparation, when your brand will start to become a reality. Your target audience will eventually begin to resonate, one person at a time. Word of mouth will activate, hype will ramp up, and you will finally arrive at a tipping point. It is there that you will begin growing at an exponential rate and the wheel will become self-sustaining.

What do you do then? Do not let up. I've worked with many artists who grind it out for more than a decade to secure a record deal, and once they get it, their mind-set shifts to *I've made it*. Well, yes, you should enjoy the hell out of such a feat, but no, you have *not made it*.

Each big break is just another beginning.

Keep pushing.

YOUR BRAND MATRIX

You have arrived at your beginning, and you are ready. Now is the time to develop your own brand statement from an authentic brand identity. Before we start, go back and review the exercises you've completed and the notes you have jotted down. Remember your purpose, strengths, defining characteristics, and target audience. Grab a pen and paper and remain conscious of the benefits of a positive mind-set to enhance open-mindedness and creativity.

If you feel you are skimming too close to the surface and need help to dig deeper, please visit my website at laurabull.com and download the *Brand Matrix Workbook* from the *All Access* area (password: clover). There you will find a complete workbook that includes each exercise from this book along with an intense identity-forming questionnaire. Together these printable tools will aid in your self-examination and brand objectivity.

As we move through these steps, creating your brand together, please remember to take your time and be completely honest. No one will see this information except you, unless, of course, you choose to share it. Beware of accidental embellishments or hopes for your future, as this could create a false brand. You should concentrate on who you are right now, at this moment in time, not who you want to be. The Rules of Evolution (Chapter 10) will help get you where you want to be later.

Let's begin with identifying your brand matrix. Write down ten adjectives that describe each of the following brand components. This process should be a thoughtful one, so spend a day or two if needed. Sleep on it. Get it right.

- Write ten words that describe your Product.
- Write ten words that describe your Image.
- Write ten words that describe your Personality.

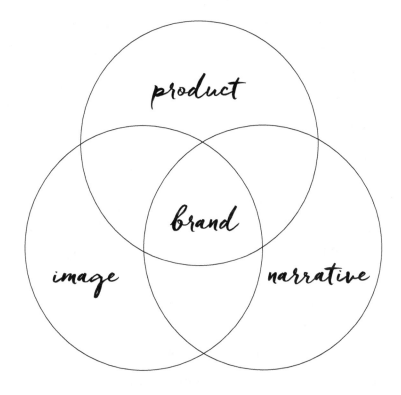

Once you have your thirty terms, it is time to find their place on the Venn diagram. Start with the first word on the Product line. Is there a similar word on the Personality/Narrative line? Is there a similar word on the Image line? If that word doesn't appear anywhere else, it belongs only in the Product circle. If it also appears in either the Narrative line or the Image line but not both it would reside in the oblong section between the center and the larger circle. If, however, your first chosen word has a counterpart on all three lines, then it belongs as a core pillar in the center! Continue this process until you have moved all your words from Image, Product, and Narrative into the diagram.

The goal is to have four to five key terms in the center of your diagram. If you have less, you need to reassess the accuracy of your original brainstorm and dig deeper. Everyone has common denominators that apply to all areas of their lives; you just need to uncover them. To seek help, ask friends and family to describe your image and personality without telling them about the Brand Matrix. On the other hand, if you have more than five core pillars, you'll need to edit down to those most important to you. Once you have just a handful of solid pillars that you feel represent you accurately it is safe to move on.

Now, grab a thesaurus and prepare to get creative. You're looking for the right words to say as much as possible with as little as possible, words that have multiple meanings when used in various ways. This is the time to find a balance between generic and specific. Think about what the deeper meanings of these words will say about you and your product.

For instance, if you find *friendly* in the center of the diagram, does this mean you are neighborly, loyal, affectionate, or social? All of these have a different connotation. If you are a politician, neighborly may be the best choice, because you are looking out for your fellow man. If you are a sportscaster, go with loyal. If you are an online blogger who focuses on new nightclubs in cities all over the world, it would be better to go with social. Get the picture?

You will likely work on your Venn diagram for several hours, if not days. Once you've finished, step back and get as objective as possible. What does your Venn diagram look like? Are you happy with it? Do these terms represent your purpose? Do they set you apart from the competition? Tweak if necessary. Remember, one unique aspect can easily set you up to win in the marketplace.

YOUR BRAND STATEMENT

You have developed your brand identity! A hearty congratulations to you! This final step in our journey together is the easy part. By putting pen to paper, and writing down a brand statement, you will gain and maintain confidence, solidify focus for time, energy, and resources, and help remove stress from future business decisions.

To create the statement, begin with writing down "[Your name] is a . . ." and follow that with an accurate depiction of your product or service. Conclude the statement by incorporating the unique characteristics and the purpose of the brand. All of your core pillars should find their way into the statement, which may be one or two sentences, but no longer. If the statement is too long, there is a lack of focus. However, feel free to make it longer for now, and edit down later.

Do you have your first attempt down? At this point, we are just trying to make sure all the key pillars are incorporated. Take a step back and read the statement a few times. Take a hard look at the words you've chosen. If they are too generic, they won't separate you from the competition; and those that are too specific may hurt your options to evolve later on. Grab the thesaurus again if you need to. Once the content is accurate, we can move on to structure.

Start to get creative with the layout and structure of the sentence.

What's the best way to convey your purpose? Is the statement written in your authentic tone and voice? It may take many pages of revisions before you land on the perfect one. Take your time and make all tweaks you feel necessary.

There are an infinite number of ways your brand statement may read, so as long as the pillars included are unique and authentic, it should be viable. The goal is to help keep you focused and confident. Once you've written your brand statement, scratched things out, rewritten, and reworked until you are happy with the final product, it is time to review your statement.

Refresher (please note that the statement I created for Oprah is not the one she created, but it includes the same pillars and therefore the same overall themes):

Oprah is an African-American lifestyle personality who promotes self-enlightenment, self-esteem, and self-efficacy through inclusion, empowerment, and spirituality.

Review your statement:

- Is this specific enough to separate you from your competition?
- Is this generic enough to allow growth and evolution over time?
- Are the core pillars highlighted?
- Can you pinpoint your purpose?
- Does this describe your product, image, and narrative?
- Is this authentic?
- Is it sellable?

If you respond with "No" to any of the above, spend more time tweaking the elements of the statement until you can respond with a "Yes" to each question. You are on your time, no one else's. You owe no one. Pause and de-stress when necessary, and above all, remain positive and keep inching forward.

Once *all* of the answers are a "Yes," CONGRATULATIONS! You are ready to embark on a marketing plan to get you into the marketplace with clarity and focus, develop a sustainable business that is poised to grow, and, best of all, live your purpose.

BRING YOUR BRAND TO LIFE

The last advice I can leave you with is to make sure you bring your brand to life in a professional fashion, and remember to think objectively when facing business decisions. You are competing with brands already successful and active in the marketplace, so look for quality over quantity and surround yourself with the very best.

Remember, you are the CEO. You are the visionary with the big ideas. No one knows your purpose and your brand better than you do. It is your responsibility to hire and steer the best team so they can deliver the best results. Be confident in who you are, bold in your abilities, and thoughtful in your purpose. Stay positive, passionate, gritty, and powerful. Believe in yourself and your dreams. Your brand is ready and so are you.

The world is waiting.

PART 4:
Resources

ALL ACCESS AT

LAURABULL.COM

●●●●

All Access at laurabull.com includes:

1. *Brand Matrix Workbook*:
   - Identity Forming Questionnaire
   - Venn diagram template
   - Each exercise from this book
2. A SWOT Analysis Worksheet with template
3. A target market analysis worksheet
4. Mood board how-to with template
5. Links to take the VIA Strengths and Grit tests
6. A link to some great speeches to identify rhetorical appeals and devices
7. Always evolving recommended reading list with links to Amazon
8. Video clips mentioned throughout the book, like "Swiftmas"

Don't forget, the secret password is clover.

Send your success stories and brand statements to @TheLauraBull and be featured on my website and social media. Let's get the word out about your brand!

RHETORIC

Check out these resources for persuasion techniques and brush up on rhetorical devices like amplification, antithesis, anaphora . . . and assonance.

1. *Rhetoric* by Aristotle
2. *Words Like Loaded Pistols: Rhetoric from Aristotle to Obama* by Sam Leith
3. *A Handlist of Rhetorical Terms* by Richard A. Lanham
4. *Lend Me Your Ears: Great Speeches in History* by William Safire
5. *Churchill: The Power of Words* by Winston Churchill and Martin Gilbert

●●●●

Be sure to check out more speeches in the All Access section!

QUICK REFERENCE

PART 1

All Celebrities ≠ Influencers

and

All Influencers ≠ Celebrities

Talent × Effort = Skill

Skill × Effort = Achievement

Passion ≠ Purpose

but

Passion + Purpose = Perseverance

PART 2

Bad Product + Bad Narrative = Failure

Good Product + Bad Narrative = Short-term Success

Bad Product + Good Narrative = Short-term Success

Good Product + Good Narrative = Long-term Success

RECOMMENDED READING

*The Happiness Advantage: The Seven Principles of Positive Psychology
    That Fuel Success and Performance at Work* by Shawn Achor
Grit: The Power of Passion and Perseverance by Angela Duckworth
Option B: Facing Adversity, Building Resilience, and Finding Joy
    by Sheryl Sandberg and Adam Grant
The Power of Story: Rewrite Your Destiny in Business and in Life
    by Jim Loehr
Digital Influencer: A Guide to Achieving Influencer Status Online
    by John Lincoln
Influence: The Psychology of Persuasion by Robert Cialdini, PhD
Whiskey in a Teacup by Reese Witherspoon
The Martha Manual: How to Do (Almost) Everything by Martha Stewart
The Gifts of Imperfection by Brené Brown
*Thrive: The Third Metric to Redefining Success and Creating a Life of
    Well-being, Wisdom, and Wonder* by Arianna Huffington
*Good to Great: Why Some Companies Make the Leap . . . and Others
    Don't* by Jim Collins
The Tipping Point: How Little Things Can Make a Big Difference
    by Malcolm Gladwell
Outliers: The Story of Success by Malcolm Gladwell
All You Need to Know About the Music Business by Donald S. Passman
Anything by Martin Seligman

ABOUT THE AUTHOR

L aura Bull spent ten years with Sony Music Entertainment where she became one of the company's youngest executives at the age of twenty-eight. During her tenure, she spearheaded artist development and marketing for globally recognized brands including Carrie Underwood, Brad Paisley, and Johnny Cash among hundreds of other artists from Arista, RCA, Columbia, Epic, and Monument records. A veteran of the music industry, she has served for more than a decade on the National Advisory Board for Musicians On Call.

She is an expert who specializes in marketing and transforming people into viable brands by offering insurmountable knowledge to teach others what it takes to become a powerful "influencer." Everyone in the marketing arena keeps discussing the power of influencers, but no one is discussing how an influencer becomes powerful. Now she redefines the term "influencer" by expanding its scope offline, highlights positive psychology principles in terms of branding, and reveals the proprietary Brand Matrix to help entrepreneurs discover their authentic and competitive brand.

A consultant and speaker, Bull has been an adjunct professor since 2013 teaching disciplines in marketing and music business at multiple colleges and universities, including SMU's Temerlin Advertising Institute. She has a BBA from Belmont University's Mike Curb School of Music Business and a Master of Liberal Studies from Southern Methodist University.

She currently resides in Dallas with her husband and daughter.